'Cos I'm A Fool

NORMAN WISDOM

'Cos I'm A Fool

with Bernard Bale

The Breedon Books
Publishing Company
Derby

First published in Great Britain by
The Breedon Books Publishing Company Limited
Breedon House, 44 Friar Gate, Derby, DE1 1DA.
1996

ISBN 1 85983 050 1

Printed and bound by Butler & Tanner Ltd., Selwood Printing Works,
Caxton Road, Frome, Somerset.

Colour separations by Colour Services, Wigston, Leicester.

Jackets printed by Lawrence-Allen, Weston-Super-Mare, Avon.

Contents

Foreword

by Dame Vera Lynn

THE very first time that I ever saw Norman Wisdom was at the Grand Theatre in Brighton, not long after he began as an entertainer. The theatre was privately-owned by Albert Rose and he had quite a few star names there. Norman was not then a star name, of course. He was a support act and we had gone along to the theatre to see some friends.

We watched the show and I just curled up at Norman's routine. He was quite unique and I can never remember laughing so much as I did that night. We met very briefly after the show and I told him how much I had enjoyed his act.

I didn't see much of him for a while after that but then, of course, his career took off and here he is today – still making people laugh in his own marvellous way.

He is a naturally funny man with a great gift for creating happiness.

Food for Thought

DON'T Laugh At Me 'Cos I'm A Fool. That song has been with me for years, I must have sung it and heard it thousands of times, yet never once has it failed to get to me. You see, people have laughed at me and I have loved every golden guffaw, every sunny smile, every precious expression that has told me I am among friends, and I value that friendship more than anything in the world.

I have said it before and I mean it – I'm just a berk really, but despite that I have made thousands and thousands of friends all over the world. Sometimes I feel that I could climb up Nelson's Column and wave to everyone just to say 'hello' and give everyone a laugh.

It gives me such a warm glow inside to know that I have so many mates. What a sharp contrast that is to my early life when I was a kid living rough. Any sign of affection was punished by my father who ruled the family with a fistful of fear. Some of you will already have heard of my earlier years, but whenever you put pen to paper there are always people and incidents which, afterwards, you wished you had included. I hope you don't mind if I relive just some of those moments of yesterday – the good and the bad. And, of course, there is so much more to tell of the more recent adventures and my thoughts on hanging up my famous 'gump' suit for the last time.

But first of all, can you imagine what it was like in Marylebone on 4 February 1915 – that was the day I was born – Norman Joseph Wisdom. Nobody noticed of course. Well, my mother Maude did – and my father Frederick almost did. My elder brother Fred knew that something was up but, since he was only two years old at the time, nobody thought to tell him too much about it. The reason why nobody else took a blind bit of notice was that they were all far more concerned with the events of World War One. Kaiser Bill had a lot to answer for and I've never really forgiven him for making my entrance into this world so unspectacular.

We actually lived at 91 Fernhead Road, Paddington, in a ground-floor flat which consisted of one bedroom, one sitting room, the kitchen and the toilet. That was it. Fernhead Road is still there, it runs from near Queens Park to Westbourne Park underground stations – and it hasn't changed that much in appearance even though it has seen a fair bit of mileage – and another world war.

My mum was a talented seamstress – she took a lot of pride in her work – and once even made a dress for Queen Mary. My dad was a chauffeur and took a lot of pride in the limos that he drove – that's probably where I inherited my passion for motors.

Although both my mum and my dad were working, for some reason we always seemed to be poor. Shoes were a luxury – and if that sounds a little trite, let me explain that my dad actually used to shave rubber off old tyres to repair the shoes that we wore. Very often, families faced with daily adversity develop a survival instinct that welds them closer together. Well, my mother did her best and I loved her dearly and Fred and I grew up to be good mates.

But my dad was a law unto himself. I don't suppose he would have lasted as a chauffeur today, he would probably have lost his licence because he liked his drink too much. Alcohol did not improve his temperament either. In fact, it made him much worse. My mother was frightened of him, not because he hit her but because he was always likely to. For Fred and me, though, it was a different story – we were rarely without bruises and I can remember my dad once throwing me across the room with such force that my head actually hit the ceiling. It was a terrible, terrible time.

My mother could not stand it for ever and, although we were very upset and stunned at the time, I could not blame her when she finally called it a day and left home. She had met another man and found refuge with him. Later they got married and remained together for the rest of their lives. Because my mother had walked out to someone else, my father was automatically given custody of us boys when the divorce finally went through.

It had been quite an experience up to then. I have vague memories World War One – I can recall seeing a German Zeppelin going over and watching it with utter fascination, only being brought out of my semi-hypnotised state when my arm was almost yanked out of its socket as my mother grabbed me and ran for cover.

I went to school at the age of four – to St Luke's Infant School to be precise. Fred and I would go hand-in-hand, dressed alike and well-behaved… well, at the start anyway. Because Fred had to look after me I was accepted into his circle of pals. They called me 'Wizzie' and treated me as one of the gang, even though I was younger and smaller. It was my first taste of camaraderie, something I would appreciate even more as I grew up.

After my mother had gone, my dad would leave us to our own devices quite a lot. He used to go away for long periods and rarely took us with him. I do remember going with him to Scotland for about eight months. He had secured a job as chauffeur to Lady Jasper Sinclair, whose husband was one of the top aristocratic businessmen in Scotland. We lived in a village called Lerags on the shores of Loch Feochan, three miles south of Oban

on the west coast. We went to Kilmore School and Fred and I
had a six-mile walk every day there and back. It was smashing.
The fresh air, the scenery, seeing sheep and cows was all
completely new to us, two little lads from the heart of West
London. We had seen horses pulling carts of course, but nothing
like this.

But it was not to last. We were all too soon on our way back
to Paddington and the life of the street-urchin, for basically that
is what we became. Left more and more to fend for ourselves we
lived on our wits and it seemed that, far from becoming easier as
we began to grow, life was becoming harder than ever.

Our existence then still involved going to school but, with dad
away so much, it was not unusual for us to be barefooted when
we sat in the classroom. Our cobbler was missing and we didn't
have his tyre-shaving skills. Our chief mates at that time were
other brothers – Wally and Arthur Nobb, Johnny Taylor who had
three other brothers whose names escape me – sorry lads! I
haven't forgotten you – just your names. Their parents were very
good to us and sometimes invited us to tea which was like
someone in the desert finding an oasis.

When dad was home we had meals, but the rest of the time
we would have done Fagin proud as Fred and I stole to eat. I'm
not exactly proud of having been a thief but in those days the
survival instinct overcame moral conscience. We used to nick
stuff from market stalls and displays outside shops – but only
food, and only what we needed.

Other pastimes included hunting for cigarette ends which we
then smoked almost as a gang ritual. We all pretended to enjoy it
but secretly we all felt pretty sick but didn't want to admit it. My
favourite pastime was playing football – I was as mad keen on
sport then as I am today. Our ball would be anything from a
pebble to a screwed-up newspaper, and we would play all day
given the chance. I still have a scar from those early soccer days.
Regrettably it was not gained with honour from a death-defying
flying header or a last-ditch heroic tackle. No, I was actually

retrieving our 'ball' from over a wall and impaled my hand on a six-inch nail when a copper yelled at me. Amazingly I did not catch some dire disease from the wound – must have been more hygienic in those days!

When all this was reaching a climax I was approaching the age of ten. I was growing up a street-wise little guy who already knew what it was like to break the law, go hungry and have a punch-up.

My mother had not totally vanished and we used to meet her in secret every now and then. Usually she would wait at the school gates to spend a few minutes with us. My tenth birthday was memorable because my mum bought me a small bike. I was thrilled to bits because it was the first thing that was actually mine. We never had toys. When my dad saw it I made the mistake of telling him that Mum had given it to me. He smashed it to pieces and gave me a good hiding when I cried.

Time went on and I started to earn a few coppers by carrying baggage for passengers at Paddington Station. Then I accidentally discovered a dodge that raked in a bit of cash with very little effort. I ran into a cycle being ridden by a well-dressed lady and was knocked flying. I sat on the ground nursing my bruises and making a bit of noise and the lady placated me by giving me a sixpenny piece. I suddenly realised that I had a 'nice little earner', and for the next few Saturday mornings I gathered in a few bob by being spectacularly sent spinning through the air by cyclists and yelling the place down until they shut me up with some coins. Funny how money can ease pain so quickly. Unfortunately an observant policeman watched me for a couple of Saturdays and sent me packing with a flea in my ear and a footprint on my backside.

Even my dad realised that his sons were turning into a couple of potential hoodlums, so he farmed us out – quite literally. We were sent to Roe Green in Hertfordshire to live with guardians because his work took him away so much. The Denmarks lived on a farm and to Fred and me it was almost like being back in

Scotland. We were surrounded by cows, goats, chickens, pigs, ducks and grass. And school, at Hatfield, was a three-mile walk just as it had been at Oban.

We loved it. The Denmark family did their best for us. I learned how to milk cows and goats by hand and we helped with feeding and taking care of the animals. I even enjoyed going to school there... well mostly! There was one teacher who had it in for me and broke my finger when he hit my hand with a blackboard ruler.

Our happiness was to be fairly short-lived at Roe Green. Dad was paying five shillings a week for the Denmarks to give us a home but he fell behind with the payments. Even that might have been tolerable but Fred and I gave our hosts a lot of headaches, too, because we were so well-steeped in the street-life survival ways of London and I'm afraid we were often in trouble for nicking fruit from orchards and the such-like.

Our next 'home' was in Kent – Isleworth Walk, Deal, to be exact. It didn't take long for our new family to sort us out – or rather, sort me out. They kept Fred and chucked me out! I was quickly found a place in nearby Walmer where Mr and Mrs Blanche of Downs Road became my guardians. They were very good for me as they were firm but understanding. I got quite a few clips around my ears but I deserved them and gradually the time-span between my ear-warmings grew longer and longer. Once again dad failed to keep up the payments – but this time the Blanches let me stay.

I was allowed to go baggage-carrying at Deal Station, I used to see Fred all the time and, at school, I began to develop an aptitude for art. I even won a school prize for a watercolour landscape. Me! The urchin from Paddington joining the ranks of Renoir and Constable! Mind you, it wasn't the last time that a constable was to play a part in my life!

The Canada Road School was also a paradise for me because it had a great sports record and really encouraged its pupils to have a go. I didn't need much encouragement. I loved all sports and still do. Football, cricket, gymnastics, running, tennis – you name it. If the school did it – I was first on the list.

I joined the Sea Scouts and once again enjoyed a special camaraderie... especially when we were locked into another survival battle – this time against the mighty ocean. *The Sea Shall Not Have Them*, *Above Us The Waves*, *The Cruel Sea*, were just three great films which later dramatised the true British stiff upper-lip approach to a life on the ocean wave. My heart swelled with the tide when I was in the Sea Scouts, even if our battle with the briny was only taking a row in a longboat hugging the Deal sea front.

It's funny how little isolated incidents in one's life become linked when you look back over the whole chain of events. I had learned the cheeky art of survival which was later to become so important to me in films. I had learned how to fall thanks to my dad and those unsuspecting cyclists. I had even learned pathos and how one quiver of a lip can get you an extra cake when a pal's mum had invited you to tea. Now, in the Sea Scouts, came another incident in my education.

I was returning to the Blanches after a Sea Scout meeting when I came across an unusual group of people outside Walmer Lifeboat Station. There was something going on and I simply had to find out what it was. Nobody took any real notice of me as I wandered among them, looking at the strange equipment that was piled on the quayside.

They were like people that I had never seen before – almost a breed of their own. Their language was different – English, but different. In short, they were actors, extras and a film crew. I was struck by their liveliness and fascinated by their work. It was the first time that I had ever encountered any element of show-business in the flesh, and the experience caused something to stir deep down inside me. I didn't recognise it at the time but it was as if I had swallowed a piece of metal and this group of people was a large magnet.

I ran home to tell Mr and Mrs Blanche and ask if I could go

back and watch them, even though it was getting late. Mrs Blanche refused point-blank so I went meekly to bed at my usual time. About an hour later I crept out of bed again, climbed out of the window and raced back to the quay.

The filming was brilliant to watch. They wanted a sea-storm scene at night – and since the sea was in a fairly relaxed mood they whipped it up a bit with the help of a rain machine. I felt as if I was being let in on a really big secret as I watched the illusion unfold that would one day thrill thousands of people sat on the edge of their seats in cinemas all over the country.

The crew didn't mind me being there. In fact they gave me a sense of belonging as they included me in their conversation, their mugs of steaming tea and their doorstep sandwiches. They filmed all night and I completely lost track of time which is why I sprinted homeward in a blind panic to avoid discovery – only to run straight into the arms of the Blanches. The smug hall clock didn't help – it chimed 7.30am as I came in through the door. I got a real dressing down from both Mr and Mrs Blanche, the latter adding to the message with a stinging slap on the ear. When I think about it, I must have perpetually had the warmest ears of any kid in Britain… I wonder if there is a place for me in the *Guinness Book of Records*.

I didn't like upsetting my lovely guardians but my experience with that film crew was one that I have always cherished. It was such a special occasion in my life and left an indelible mark. As it turned out, when it was my turn to be in front of the cameras, I sometimes came across kids just like me, and I've always tried to make sure that there was a kind word and a mug of tea for them in fond memory of that wonderful crew who opened the door a crack and gave me my first peek into the fantastic world of showbusiness that eventually became my entire life.

After that episode, life returned to normality. I continued to run errands, deliver things and carry baggage in order to earn a few bob until it was time for my next major step… leaving school.

I was 14 at the time and I was by no means work-shy. I had

learned the lesson that you don't get more out of life than you put in, so I quickly found myself a job as a delivery boy and at the same time learned yet another lesson that was to stay with me for the rest of my life. My first job was in a china shop and you may be surprised to know that not once did I ever break anything. I earned ten shillings a week, kept sixpence for myself and handed the rest over to the Blanches. I did this voluntarily because they had fed and clothed me all that time for nothing. I owed them a lot and I wanted to repay their kindness. It meant that I was still permanently skint but I felt better that I was able to show them my genuine appreciation for all that they had done for me.

Things improved a little when I successfully applied for a job at Lipton's the Grocers near the china shop. A smart delivery-bike with a big panier and the company emblem went with that job – it was a bit big for me but the manager gave me the benefit of the doubt and I became a familiar part of the local scene as I pedalled like fury to get my deliveries accomplished as quickly as possible. I took a real pride in being Deal's fastest delivery boy.

The lesson? – Well there were two really. The biggest was in relationships with people. When I was not delivering I used to be doing odd jobs around the shop. Nobody took a blind bit of notice of me. I was almost invisible unless someone wanted something and, to tell you the truth, I found that being mostly ignored like that was very hurtful. I swore that I would never knowingly ignore anyone the way that I had been at that shop, and I have always done my best to live up to that vow. If I have ever seemed to ignore you then please accept my apology – it was certainly unintentional. I would never want to make anyone feel the way I felt at that shop.

The second lesson was to be more careful when considering business moves. One day, when I was zooming along on my bike, the manager of the rival Home and Colonial Store stopped me and offered me a job with his shop. He tempted me with an offer of twelve shillings a week – that was more like it! But of course, I couldn't just graciously accept. The guile of London street-life bubbled up in me and I went to my boss at Lipton's. When I told him about the offer he agreed to match it. I couldn't leave it at that though – Oh no! Far too simple.

I belted back to Home and Colonial and told the boss that Lipton's had matched his offer. He upped the ante to fourteen shillings. I dashed back to Lipton's and excitedly told the manager the latest development – eagerly awaiting his response.

"Bye bye!" – That was all he said. Well, actually he said something like "Shove off!" but we won't go into that. Still I had a new job and a better income at Home and Colonial... for six weeks. Then they bought a van and I was out of a job.

It was only a few months since I had left school and I couldn't afford to be without a job, so I quickly made my way to the Job Centre – except that we didn't have such a posh title for it in those days – the Deal Labour Exchange was good enough. Well, I went along to exchange my redundant labour for some cash but there was not a lot doing locally for someone of my tender years and size. But then they did find something for me that sounded all right... I was to become an apprentice waiter at the Artillery Mansion Hotel in Victoria Street, London. Yes, back to dear old London town, a new challenge, twelve shillings a week and the guarantee that even though I was going to be on my own again, at least I was going to be near food!

In Search of Adventure

WHEN you've had your nose pressed up against a baker's window with the rumbling in your stomach sounding like an old boiler, it makes you think that you've really made it when you land a job that provides you with grub, your own room – even though you couldn't swing a Manx cat in it – and a uniform. I had been in uniform before of course, in the Sea Scouts, but this was a lot more posh. The jacket, trousers, waistcoat and bow-tie made me feel quite proud of myself. I would stand in front of the mirror for hours, making sure that not a hair was out of place and that my shoes were as clean and shiny as the silver tray that I was expected to carry.

After a couple of weeks I had enough money to buy my very first suit – it was second-hand of course, but it was mine. I even invested in some new shoes and a silver-grey trilby. I was a dapper little so-and-so and bordered on smugness. You know what they say about pride – well, guess what? I had a problem with the lift shaft! No, it wasn't me that fell – it was the tray of left-over breakfasts that I had just collected from a room on the fifth floor. It slid off my shoulder when I looked down the shaft to see where the lift had gone.

The head-waiter was a perfect gentleman and kindly said, "Norman, if I get you another job – will you leave?"

How about that for a polite way of giving someone the boot!

True to his word he did find me another job – at the Ladies Forum Club, near Hyde Park Corner. It wasn't half as interesting as it sounds though – it was all Forum and no ladies, if you see what I mean.

But this new job threw me into two experiences that could have been scripts from the films that were to come later. There were lots of boys and girls working in the many hotels and clubs in the area and, of course, we got to know each other quite well. One of our recreations was going for dancing lessons. It was the first time that I had ever done such a thing and I enjoyed it very much. It opened up a new talent to me, and was one that I was able to put to good use later.

I also fell in love. My interest in the opposite sex had been stirred – if not shaken – while I was at the Ladies Forum Club. It is amazing how many of the guests neglected to block the keyholes when they were taking a bath… er, at least that's what the other lads told me. At the dancing school I met Sally. Unlike most of the other girls, Sally did not snigger because I was smaller than she was. I thought she was wonderful and one day I decided to throw caution to the wind and ask her out. She hesitated at first and pointed out that I couldn't really afford a night out on the town.

Two weeks later I had succeeded in saving what I thought would be enough and, with a delightful little laugh, Sally said 'yes' when I asked her out again. I couldn't stop grinning with joy as I got myself ready and, sure enough, there she was at our pre-arranged meeting place. We went to the pictures at the Metropole Cinema near Victoria Station. Don't ask me what we saw – I was on cloud nine – the projector could have broken down for all I knew.

I asked if she would like to eat – I had to wine and dine her you see. Mind you, I had to watch the pennies as well, so it was two teas and egg and chips twice in a nearby cafe. She seemed in a bit of a hurry and didn't finish her meal. I walked her to the bus-stop and just as we neared it the bus came. Sally smartly ran and got on it leaving me alone on the pavement, not having had the chance to say goodnight. She glanced out of the window and didn't seem at all unhappy at our parting. I saw her the next day and, as I rushed to greet her, she turned her back on me and walked away – never to speak to me again. My first pangs of love lay shattered on the ground around me and tears welled up into my eyes.

One of my page-boy pals was a Welsh lad named Joe. It was Joe who suggested that we become coalminers. I had been a page-boy for only a few weeks but was already finding it boring. The mining idea sounded more of an adventure and so I agreed. I handed in my notice, only to find that Joe had changed his mind. However, after a few days Joe changed his mind yet again and we were off to Glandwr near Cardiff – on foot!

A fortnight later, sleeping rough, we staggered into Cardiff. Joe and I then fell out after he admitted that he hadn't told his parents that we were coming – and that there probably wouldn't be a place for me at their house. We parted company and I walked into the nearest building to try to get a job... it was the Hippodrome Theatre.

"I want to get into showbusiness!" I told the manager as I broke into a sort of soft-shoe shuffle while singing *I'm Forever Blowing Bubbles*. His look of surprise was not one of admiration – but he was not unkind. He suggested that it would require rather more than I appeared to be offering. Perhaps I would like to try again when I had developed a real act. Years later I was Top of the Bill at that theatre, and I would dearly have loved to have shaken that manager's hand and jogged his memory – but regrettably he was no longer there and I never did see him again.

I had walked to Cardiff in search of work and adventure and I had been disappointed... at least, so I thought. But, of course, Cardiff is famous for its docks – that noisy gateway to the world.

Inexorably, I found myself drawn to this kaleidoscope of clanking chains, groaning cranes and vocal strains.

As I wandered around, a dockyard gate guard told me to clear off but, as I turned to go, another man – a foreman – stopped me and asked where I had come from. When I told him London, he and his mates burst out laughing – until he looked at the soles of my shoes – there weren't any. Next thing I knew I was sitting with the group sharing their tea and sandwiches. I felt that I had been in this situation before as, of course, I had – although I hadn't felt so desperate when I was among the members of that film-crew back in Deal.

That foreman turned out to be a real pal. He took me to a captain he knew and got me a job as a cabin-boy on the *Maindy Court*. Where were we going? That's exactly what I asked. Quite nonchalantly the captain replied, "Argentina!"

Argentina! That was a bit further from home than the Ladies Forum Club. It was at that point that I realised that home was really wherever I happened to be at any particular time. The *Maindy Court* was now my home. I had a bed, food and an income – and also the adventure that I had craved. I also had a mountain of potatoes. Yes, that was my first task – spud-bashing. It wasn't going to be my last encounter with peeling King Edwards either.

Life aboard an 8,000-ton cargo ship, bound for a place I had only heard about in geography lessons, was certainly something new. In all, we were to be on a round trip lasting five months. My wages were ten shillings a week with very little to spend it on. I worked from six in the morning until around midnight and most of the time I was completely tired out. I was sea-sick at first – but then I became too fatigued to vomit and so my body decided to settle for being shattered nearly all the time.

Apart from once getting a punch in the face from the enormous first-mate, I got on really well with the rest of the crew whose favourite leisure pursuit was boxing. Between throwing scraps to sea birds and marvelling at dolphins I used to spend a

lot of time at these impromptu boxing tournaments on board
ship. I even started to take part. The crew gave me lots of advice
but finally decided that I was a 'natural'. Being small, and light on
my feet, I kept out of trouble and could land a few good 'uns of
my own, cheered on by the crew.

When we finally docked in Buenos Aires some of the crew
decided to take me out on the town. First stop was a local fun-
fair and guess what we found there – that's it! A boxing booth.
Open to challengers was a plug-ugly gorilla of a man who looked
as if he could eat iron-railings like spaghetti. The idea was that
you could earn a pound for every round that you lasted with this
ape-man, and if you lasted for all three you'd be richer by five
pounds... ten week's wages! I had no intention of stepping into
the ring with that mountain of bone and muscle of course, but,
as it happened, the choice had already been made for me. Later
on I realised that the whole point of my being taken out 'on the
town' was for the sole purpose of getting me into the ring at this
very well-known boxing booth.

They assured me that if I remembered 'all that they had taught
me' and stayed nimble, the monster in the opposite corner would
never lay a glove on me. "You can't let the ship down," they said
– and I was inevitably shamed into it. They cheered like mad
when I stepped into the ring and even louder when the bell rang
to start the round. I looked at my snarling opponent and then at
the referee... What referee? There wasn't one – only a time-
keeper outside the ring.

Well, that booth bruiser fetched me a fourpenny one and
down I went. The crew howled for me to stay down until the
count of nine. They needn't have bothered – I felt like staying
down until ninety-nine! But I did get up and somehow managed
to stagger through the rest of the round. I was a pound richer but
if it had been waved in front of me I would have thought it was
two, so dazed was I. The second round saw me on the canvas
again. I thought I was boxing the rear end of a mule.

I don't remember much more except that I had one eye closed

and blood coming from my other one – and my nose, and my mouth. They told me afterward that after getting clobbered yet again in the third I suddenly turned into a whirlwind, dancing around the ring and throwing punches like a machine gun. I never actually hurt the Argentinian but it did stop him from finishing me off. One thing that I do remember is the little smile he gave me and the wave at the end of that fight.

I often think of that man. Was he just a bruiser with nothing else going for him? That final smile suggested something else. Perhaps a man feeding his family in the only way he knew how… who knows?

After I had cleaned up I went to rejoin my shipmates. They'd disappeared – and they had taken my winnings with them to celebrate without me.

That wasn't my only adventure on that voyage. I ran into a political riot in Buenos Aires and had to run for cover, I had to wrestle with a Greek engineer to ward off his amorous advances toward me, and then, when I visited a 'lady' who, the crew assured me, would initiate me in the ways of love, she gave me a clout that my Argentinian sparring-partner would have been proud of. We fell foul of the notorious Bay of Biscay and my fatigue was pushed back into second place by my sea-sickness for a while. There were other escapades, not the least being a time when I accidentally allowed a stray wave to mix with the pea soup I was carrying. The officers didn't seem to mind – they just took a little less salt than usual.

After one final call to unload some grain at Rotterdam we docked back in Cardiff. Since the *Maindy Court* was not due to sail again for some months, I once again found myself at a loose end and in need of work. However, I was nearly 15 now, had some cash in my pocket and a few tales to tell. I almost swaggered into the Cardiff Labour Exchange.

While they were finding me a job they sent me to a hostel and I was there on Christmas Day 1929. By lunch-time everyone had gone. The cook shoved my meal toward me, muttered something about a Merry Christmas, and then went home to her family. I looked around and, apart from the plate of sausage and mash in front of me, I was completely alone. It wasn't that it was Christmas, it was the loss of the company and camaraderie that had become so important to me. I would have given anything to have heard just one voice – any voice. Like my ship's officers, I didn't need any salt on my food that day, my tears did it for me.

The Labour Exchange did their best to find me a job. They even sent me to a pub in Henley-on-Thames where it turned out that the landlord wanted a barman. He took one look at me and angrily sent me packing. He didn't think that I was up to hauling barrels about. Maybe he was right. I hitched a lift to London and decided to visit my grandparents. They were less than thrilled to see me and gave me the address of my dad – their son – in Earl's Court.

A lady answered the door and introduced herself – Mrs Wisdom. I explained who I was and she invited me in to wait until my dad returned from work. It had been four years since I had seen him and, as far as I was concerned, the past was the past. He seemed to have settled down in a pleasant home with a pleasant new wife – not like my mum of course, but pleasant all the same.

At last he returned and when I heard his voice outside the room I felt an overwhelming joy. Tears came to my eyes and as he came into the room my voice cracked. All I could say was "Dad," and hold out my hand.

"Get out!" Those were the only two words he spoke and his face remained totally dispassionate as he held the door wide.

"I'll never see you again," I said as I stumbled through that door, but there wasn't the slightest flicker of emotion from him. I never did see him again. He eventually died, of course, but I never knew the details. I know that probably sounds extremely callous but it wasn't quite the way it seems. I often thought about my dad and desperately wished that things could have been different. But I lost all contact after that time, and never heard any more about him until it was too late.

After that final encounter with my dad I felt very unwanted and wandered the streets of London as a vagrant. I spent the next month living in shop doorways and near warm-air vents, fraternising with the 'Knights of the Road' who had foresaken their country haunts for the warmer climate of London, where winter could be survived thanks to those price-conscious menus of tea and coffee stalls – and the generosity of hotel dustbins.

Cinemas provided great daytime refuge as their exit doors were often ajar – and inside were warm seats, hot and cold water and entertainment. By dodging into the toilets when the lights came up I found that you could remain in the cinema nearly all day.

There were also a few helpful people about. I never begged or asked for anything but sometimes people would offer you things quite unsolicited. The owner of a coffee stall near Victoria Station was one of those people. Every night he gave me a hot pie and a mug of Bovril. Then one night he gave me a really tremendous gift – some genuine advice.

"Why don't you join the Army?" He said. "They take lads of fourteen in the Army band."

I protested that I didn't know anything about music but he just grinned. "Pretend you do! They'll teach you once you're in."

I couldn't sleep that night. I turned it over and over in my mind and something kept telling me that it was the right thing to do. After all, looking around me, what had I got to lose?

That well-meaning advice turned out to be more than just an escape from the downward spiral of vagrancy, more than just a new job in the Army. It was the first step on the road that led me to nights at the London Palladium, Broadway, films, fame and, dare I say it, a little fortune.

The next day I went to the Army recruitment office in Whitehall and was allowed in even though the office was actually closed that day. They gave me a bed and a meal for the night and the following day I met the bandmaster. Well, at four feet, ten and a half inches, and five stone and nine pounds, I wasn't exactly destined for the Grenadier Guards.

The bandmaster eyed me up and down and fired a few questions at me. I did my best but my musical education was pretty conspicuous by its absence.

"You don't know the first thing about music do you boy?" He demanded.

"No sir, I'm sorry," I managed to stammer, and turned to leave. Suddenly a thought came into my mind – what did I have to lose?

"I'm sorry to have wasted your time sir. Being honest, I was hoping to bluff my way in and then learn." I cringed, waiting for the expected blast.

The bandmaster relaxed. "Give me your address and I'll put you on the waiting list."

Address? What address? I gulped and took a gamble. I gave him the only address that I could think of – 21 Shirland Road, Kilburn. That was the address at which my dad's parents lived. After my last reception there I wasn't sure how helpful they would be – but I didn't have a lot of choice.

Before going to see my grandparents again I called in at the nearest Labour Exchange – and, to my delight, I landed a job as a page-boy at the Marble Arch Pavilion, which later became the Odeon, one of the biggest and best cinemas in the West End. I was to receive £1 a week and a uniform. When they heard that, my grandparents agreed to let me stay for a while and they did try to make me feel at home as best they could.

The cinema was terrific. One of my jobs was to escort VIP guests who were attending premières and special functions. I even got a kiss from Joan Crawford one night. Also my musical education started at the Pavilion. Reginald Foort was resident organist and I used to hang around while he practised. In fact, he taught me something very important. One morning I asked him why he kept playing this particular piece over and over.

"You have to keep at it until you get it absolutely right," he told me. It was another piece of advice that has since proved so invaluable to me. Since then I have always made a point of practising until I have achieved as near to perfection as I am ever likely to.

I'd almost forgotten about the Army when an envelope arrived at Shirland Road addressed to me. The letter informed me that I had been accepted as a drummer-boy. I was to become a member of the King's Own Royal Regiment based at Lichfield in Staffordshire. I was thrilled by the letter and, as it subsequently turned out, I was not disappointed either. I reported immediately and spent my first three months learning the rudiments of music and in particular how to play the drum – military style.

It was Utopia for me – new mates, an adventure, music, some-where to live and regular pay. Because I was in the music section there was not too much square-bashing. I was kept busy with the skin-bashing though and the first three months went like lightning. I had a fortnight's leave and if I was happy with life it was nothing compared to my next bit of joy. A little parcel was delivered to my grandparents' address. Inside was a hairbrush, but on the back was the address of the sender – MY MUM! I hadn't seen her for nearly five years and I couldn't stop laughing out of sheer happiness.

Within the hour I was on my way to the address in Peckham. Any passer-by must have thought that I was a head-case – I just couldn't stop grinning. When I arrived at the address I found that it actually belonged to my Auntie May. My mother was living in Russell Square. My aunt sent my mother a telegram and made me wait with her. Sure enough, as day drew into evening, there was a knock at the door and there stood my lovely mum. She looked great. We threw our arms round each other and just stayed like that for ages.

Well, we caught up on the missing years although I missed out some of the experiences because I did not want her to be troubled. She was very happy with her new husband – Sydney

Poulton – and was getting on really well. She looked it too. She didn't knock my new Army career but thought that I could do better.

"You used to be good at drawing, Norman. Why not try to be an architect? Have a bit of ambition, dear."

She didn't understand how happy I was in the Army and how much it had done for me. I loved my mum and guessed that she knew best – so when she offered to buy me out, I didn't resist. She travelled up to Lichfield with me, handed over £35 and made me a free agent again. Within a week she had got me a job as a trainee draughtsman at the Trust Concrete Steel Company. She also took me on a bit of a shopping spree for some new clothes and that was it – she had set me up for a new life, a fresh start.

I appreciated it, I really did. I turned up for work at my new job – and lasted about two hours. I hated it and had to walk out. I didn't have the education for it and I didn't have the required plum in my mouth to identify with the other 'chaps' in the office. I was a square peg and no mistake.

As I stood on the Embankment looking at the Thames, I saw the flowing water, the barges and the people afloat and it took me back to the *Maindy Court* and her crew, and then back to my pals in the Army. That camaraderie, that sense of belonging and that spirit of adventure. I knew I could never find these things in the office job that my mother had so lovingly found for me.

I had to be honest with myself and say that while there was nothing wrong with a nine-to-five office job, it was just not for me. I turned away from the Thames and marched along the Embankment to Whitehall – and the Army recruiting office.

The interview was quite simple this time, although I didn't let on that I had been in before less than six months ago. It was a different bandmaster but he asked the same questions – this time I knew the answers.

The interview with my mum was not so easy. I felt bad after all she had done and she was a bit upset. But in the end honesty won the day. I explained to her how I really felt. I opened my heart to her and, at the end of it all, amid hugs and kisses and promises to keep in touch, she finally gave me her blessing.

I was back in the Army – this time with the 10th Hussars – and a whole new world was opening up ahead of me.

You're In
The Army
Now

AH YES, the Army! I had already learned much from life. My encounter with the film crew, the ability to earn an extra morsel by using my 'hang-dog' look, the cheers of the crowd in Argentina, learning a script by sitting in a cinema all day watching the same film over and over again. All these were parts of my education – gems that would later prove to be so priceless in my ultimate career. The icing on the cake came in the shape of the Army.

I had not been back in for long when the word rushed around the troops that we were going to India. Most of the lads had never been further than Clacton, and my voyage on the *Maindy Court* had made me a well-seasoned traveller in the eyes of all the others. I became a really popular bloke as they approached me with all sorts of questions. I assumed that India would be near enough the same as Argentina, only with saris instead of ponchos. When I think back I talked some real rubbish as I held court in my guise as the 'Old Man of the Sea'.

For nearly three weeks I was at Aldershot going through

exactly the same things as I had learned in basic training at Lichfield. We knew that the Hussars were destined for India – but we didn't know when. When it did happen, it happened very quickly. The call came, then the injections – Ouch! – just enough time for me to get word to my mum and the next thing that I knew was that I was marching up the gangplank of the SS *Southampton*, together with my kit-bag, bound for a six-week voyage on the ocean blue. I'm proud to report that, this time, I was not sea-sick which once again did my street cred – or ship cred – a power of good.

It might sound a little rude to say that when you're sailing to India you can smell it long before you can see it, but I'm not being at all disrespectful. It was a bit like sniffing the air in a busy town and following your nose to the nearest Indian restaurant. Your taste-buds go on red alert and your stomach shouts 'let me at it'. It was just like that as we approached Calcutta.

It was wonderful! The sheer mass of people, the incredible aromas, and the noise of a million chattering voices was a total culture shock after six weeks at sea. No sooner had we set foot in this strange new land, however, than we were whisked on to a hissing steam train for a 600-mile trip in a microwave. Most of the time we rattled through desert and scrubland and it was so hot that you could have fried an egg on a bald head.

Lucknow is in the more northerly province of Oudh, and is set on the inviting River Gunti. When we stepped down off the train we received yet another culture shock. What I saw made the back streets of Paddington look like Pall Mall. Once again the place was absolutely teeming with humanity but a large proportion of them were beggars, pathetically reaching out with withered limbs in the hope of attracting a stray coin. The whole place looked as if it suffered daily earthquakes. Even the major buildings were little more than tumbledown shacks.

Business was rife – among other things. Everyone seemed to have something to sell. The whole place was a tip – but once again there were those delightful smells, a constant excited chatter, splashes of colour from the saris, the shop-fronts and the vehicles – even the donkeys were decorated. Then another thing struck me. All these people were intent on eking out their meagre living as best they could. It was an absolute contrast to my surroundings as a page-boy – but these people had a common bond. They all had smiling faces, they all laughed together… and how cheerful they were. Despite everything that life seemed to throw at them they were happy, and, as my head hit the pillow for my first night at the garrison, so was I.

Of course, there was a bit more than playing music to being in the Hussars – but we'll come to the horses… yes, HORSES… later. I learned to trot before I even got near a horse. Getting acclimatised and getting used to the food and water meant that we all learned to trot – some even broke into a gallop – to the latrines. The dreaded 'Delhi Belly' took its toll, but after a week or two we all began to feel pretty pleased with ourselves. Some of the lads were a bit homesick and, of course, I often thought of my family back home in dear old Blighty – but I had become accustomed to being far away from them and therefore did not suffer as much as most of the others.

I love music – of all kinds – and I had quickly come to love being in the Army. We were given regular pep talks reminding us of where we were and exactly what our conduct should be. I did not need much reminding. I was enjoying myself and I didn't want to spoil it. Back in Europe, and the United States, that inevitable spiral had begun which was to culminate in the Great Depression of the 1930s. But for me, here in India, life could hardly have been better. I was as happy as a crocodile in the Ganges.

Mr Roberts – Robbo to us when he was out of earshot – was our bandmaster. I was a bit taken aback when he called me in one day, stood me to attention and began to run his finger over my lips. Thoughts of that Greek engineer came flooding back and I nearly scarpered there and then. As it happened he was merely checking the shape of my lips to weigh up which instrument would be the best for me to concentrate on. I must admit that, later, I felt a bit bad about my suspicions because Robbo turned out to be a really decent bloke who played a major part in my musical education.

"Clarinet for you my lad," he said, and I was issued with a real beauty. But we all – or nearly all anyway – had to learn the trumpet as well so that we could sound all the usual *Regimental Posts*. I say 'nearly all' because we had one chap named Simpson on drums who had a hare-lip, and if we'd had to wait for him to sound the *Last Post* before we could get off to sleep, none of us would have got a wink!

Although much of our time was taken up with practice and hard work, we managed to have a lot of fun as well. One incident, however, turned out to be very far from funny. I was on 'Trumpet Duty' in the guardhouse, which meant that I had to stay there for 24 hours and sound the various calls at the appropriate times. The idea being that there was a trumpeter on call at all times in case of any emergency. You had sleep time and could really do as you liked providing you remained at the guard-house for your tour of duty.

Well, one particular night, I was there with three other blokes and we decided to have a game of cards. While I got the pack ready the others finished off whatever they were doing. One of them, Mike, had been cleaning his rifle and was just preparing it for action when there was a loud bang. He had accidentally fired it and the poor bloke had put a bullet through his own head. He died instantly. We, of course, were shocked rigid and I was sick for days afterwards. It was a truly awful thing to have happened.

While we were still learning to tell the difference between our flats and our sharps, us junior musicians were often left behind when the band went away to perform a concert or some other official engagement. During one of these respites I had a rummage around the music store and discovered an old, dusty, cobweb-covered xylophone. To me it was an object of real beauty. I cleaned and polished it until it shone and found that it was in very good condition. I secretly set about learning how to play and, by the time the senior band returned to barracks, I was able to play a couple of numbers.

At the end of our three-hour long practice sessions with the band, the bandmaster was in the habit of asking if anyone would like to select a couple of numbers to finish off with. One morning, shortly after the band had returned from a month-long engagement, the opportunity arose to spring my surprise. No sooner had the bandmaster made his expected request then up went my hand.

"Excuse me sir, could we play *Snowflakes*?"

The bandmaster must have thought that the sun had got to me. Not only was *Snowflakes* more of a Christmas number suitable for Britain, but the nearest thing to a snowflake we would be able to see was a few thousand feet up in the Himalayas. Eyeing me suspiciously he spoke as if he were speaking to someone mentally deranged. "Wisdom, *Snowflakes* happens to be a xylophone solo."

My grin must have confirmed his suspicions.

"All right Wisdom, go and get it!"

I was off in a flash, returning in minutes pushing the gleaming xylophone like some hospital trolley bed. The rest of the band sat back while I did my stuff with *Snowflakes*. I finished and threw a hopeful glance at the bandmaster. My heart sank – his face was stern and impassive – you could have heard a pin drop. Suddenly the silence was shattered as the band began to cheer and applaud. Even bandmaster Roberts joined in and, from then on, *Snowflakes* became a regular part of the band's repertoire and I had made it into the band proper.

Of course that wasn't the end of it. You know what I'm like – following the success with the xylophone I just had to have a go at something else. I realised that we didn't have a solo vocalist, even though we all joined in the choruses of sea shanties and similar numbers. I volunteered to have a go and, once again, bandmaster Roberts gave me an audition. He was impressed enough to let me sing at the next concert engagement as well as keeping my xylophone solo and my parts with the clarinet.

The solos went well in the sea shanties and they too became a regular feature of the concerts. I was lapping up the applause at every gig and, although I didn't realise it at the time, I had been really bitten by the showbiz bug. It is a creature from which there is no escape. Once you have been bitten there is no cure. For the first time in my life I was getting applause for the things that I enjoyed doing. Fortunately it didn't go to my head – but it did go to my heart. At the risk of sounding a bit soppy I was beginning to feel the love of an audience and in return I fell head-over-heels in love with them.

Don't get the impression that all we did in those days was sit on our backsides playing music all the time. Oh no, far from it. A few years ago there was an excellent television series *It Ain't 'Arf 'Ot Mum*. It depicted the comic adventures of a military concert party in India and it brought back more than a few memories of many of my own escapades. But there was a serious side to life in the Army as well as a comic one. It was the Army that furthered my general education, gave me discipline, physical fitness, how to appreciate a good curry, taught me such skills as map-reading and shooting – I became a marksman by the way – and even taught me to speak properly. I spent a lot of time mixing with officers and they introduced me to a completely new letter in my alphabet. The letter 'Aitch' which was sounded by a sharp puff of air. All those years I 'ad combed my 'air wiv an 'airbrush – but now a whole new world was being opened up to me and I felt well able to hold my own with all those lads from 'Arrow an 'Heton. A while later, when I saw my mum again, she just couldn't believe how 'posh' I had become.

There was something else that the Army taught me – how to fall off a horse. We all had to learn to ride and so I was intro-duced to Sixie, a lovely chestnut mare who was to become my constant companion. Well, as constant as I could manage con-sidering that I had never ridden a horse in my life. I have to admit that it was fear at first sight. I looked up at her with my knees doing a fair impression of my xylophone solo. She looked down at me with a knowing smile on her face.

"Be gentle with me," I pleaded as she chewed on her hay. She tossed her head. I'm sure she must have been thinking, "I've got a right one here."

As it happens she was gentle with me and, after my first lesson in the saddle, my confidence was soaring, my knees were aching and my bum seemed to have disappeared – well it had gone numb anyway.

Our instructor, Sergeant-Major Jaye, was something of a dare-devil – the sort of lunatic who is invaluable to the film industry for performing all those death-defying stunts. He soon had us adopting his suicidal approach to riding and Sixie came into her own as we galloped backwards and forwards over the roughest of rough ground as part of our equestrian education.

"If you ever find yourself in combat on horseback you won't be able to select nice little paths or well-trimmed hurdles!" The sergeant-major would bellow. He was right, of course, and, as time went by, my bum became less numb and reappeared. There were times, however, when I wished it was still oblivious to the aches and pains of that hard leather saddle.

Eventually I became an astronaut! Now, you might wonder, how could a soldier serving in the 10th Hussars, in India, in the 1930s, possibly become an astronaut. I couldn't have done it on my own, of course, and it was Sixie who assisted in my first 'launching'. There we were, in full flight in the wake of madcap Sergeant-Major Jaye, when Sixie found herself hurtling toward a whacking great hedge. She was no coward but this was one that she really didn't fancy. On went the brakes, all four of them, and as her front and rear-end concertina'd, I found myself launched into the air. It was the Wisdom Space Mission.

I did keep hold of the reins and therefore found myself water-skiing on land as Sixie did her level best to get away from the scene of her recent embarrassment. By the time she stopped my poor bum had disappeared again. Sixie merely tugged at the grass and gave me one of those looks that only a horse can give. It was as if she was saying, "Well, what did you expect? If I was that good they would have entered me in the Grand National!"

The rest of the troop were howling with laughter and it sparked off another idea in the mind of Sergeant-Major Jaye. He had the brainwave of putting on equestrian displays. Guess who was chosen to play the stooge – the little bloke who keeps falling off? Yes, you've got it – Norman.

I didn't mind in the least. In fact I was all for it and began suggesting all sorts of stunts which, of course, were turned down because the whole thing had to remain within the bounds of military decorum and could not be an excuse to put on a circus. Falling off into a haystack was deemed to be sufficient and I got plenty of laughs and applause when it happened during our displays.

Apart from the riding I continued in my love of other sports. I enjoyed a game of soccer, cricket, bicycle polo or anything else that was on offer. I started boxing again and eventually became flyweight champion of the British Army in India – a title that I successfully defended until I returned, undefeated, to Britain.

It was boxing that led me to another great discovery. I was in the barrack-room doing a bit of shadow boxing when I started messing about pretending that I had an invisible opponent who was giving as good as he got. I was punched here and there, hit back, ducked, got knocked over, got up, landed a couple and then got dumped on my backside again.

My mates in the barrack-room were in hysterics and suddenly something went 'Ping!' I realised that my music, my love of an audience, singing and all the rest of it could combine forces just so long as I had something special to offer – and this was it – comedy!

I had a number of other Army experiences in India that helped colour my career there. I did, like most people, get into trouble now and then. I didn't get the wrong side of the glasshouse bars, but I did get handed some rotten jobs as a result of some of my misdemeanours. I was once made to dig a grave six feet down, six feet long and three feet across – and then given a dead mouse to be buried in it. And, of course, I sampled the delights of 'jankers' on more than one occasion.

I could never resist messing about, even on such things as drill parade, and my mates would almost suffer apoplexy as they tried to contain their laughter, while the drill sergeant would have steam coming out of his ears – never quite sure if I was acting the fool or was naturally stupid.

Strange as it may seem, the Army also made me abandon regular drinking habits and smoking. I know, it's usually the other way about, but for me, as a hyperactive little guy playing football, clarinet and the fool, I realised what a health hazard I had created for myself. I have rarely smoked since and my drinking has been very moderate.

I seemed to have little time for the opposite sex. It wasn't that I had no interest but most time that was left free for myself seemed to be spent spark out in the barrack-room. I met girls of course but, although chatting with them was a very pleasant experience, I was extremely awkward and shy.

In February 1936 I was on my way home. My 21st birthday was spent aboard ship during that five-week voyage. India had been quite an experience, from the discovery of that dust-covered xylophone in the music store to the odd experience of being in an earthquake in Lucknow where you realised how powerless you were against the mighty forces of nature.

Blighty was beckoning and I was on my way home, a wiser young man with much to thank the Army for. However, I knew that it was time to move on and see what the world had in store for me. I had been saving and now I had enough to buy myself out for the second time. I had this mysterious 'something' that was nagging at me. I wanted to continue with my music and I kept reliving the sounds of applause, cheers and, most of all, laughter. I couldn't understand why – maybe Civvie Street would have all the answers.

Stagestruck

WHEN I travelled out to India I had been an average London lad who didn't even know what an 'Aitch' was. I had known of places like 'Ackney and 'Ammersmiff but, since I had spent so much time with the officers, I had now discovered Harrow and Heton. My mum had waved goodbye to her cockney son and soon she would be saying 'hello' to this posh little twerp who raised his little finger when he drank a cup of tea. My mum couldn't stop laughing when she saw all the changes in me.

As soon as I arrived back in England, I went straight to see her and her husband and found that there was a room waiting for me at their home in Sherrick Green Road. I had saved enough money to buy myself out of the Army and I was also able to pay my mother back for the time she bought me out the first time. Now that I was out, the burning question at the front of my brain was – now what?

The all-important thing was income, and I was prepared to do just about anything – so I took a leaf out of my dad's book. After a few lessons from my mum I was able to drive and I took a job with 'Speedy Service' – a private-hire firm based in Kilburn. Even now, I still have a bit of a mania for cars and if I could pinpoint where that started, I am sure it was at that private-hire firm when I fell in love with my Wolseley car.

The job went fine, but I still wanted a bit of extra cash so, when I saw an card in the window of Willesden telephone

exchange advertising for part-time night-shift telephone oper-
ators, I saw a way of adding to my income. With my best 'officer's'
voice I walked the interview and began working there for three
nights a week – all the time continuing with my daytime job in
the Wolseley. I was enjoying life – and it was about to get even
better.

I don't know how many people fall in love through the steamy
aroma of a fish and chip shop – but I did. I used to nip in for my
'cod and two penn'orth' before going on to work at the nearby
telephone exchange. There, amid the steaming batter and the
newspaper wrapping, was a lovely, smiling young lady with
blonde curly hair. Her name was Doreen – the most beautiful
sound I had ever heard. Immediately we met there was a plaice
for her in my heart. I always wanted her to take her time in
wrapping my fish and chips so that I could talk to her a little
longer each time I went in there. I used a few corny lines and she
bunged me a few extra chips – What a courtship!

We started going out together and within a few months I had
popped the big question. She accepted and we were married in
the church at Willesden Green. There might well have been
more salt and vinegar than hearts and roses but we were both
happy.

World War Two changed everyone's life – mine included.
Because of my work at the Willesden telephone exchange, I was
considered to be in a vital communications job and therefore was
not called up for military service, even though I had Army experience. Each night the bombing raids swept London and, in our
glass-roofed telephone nerve centre, we seemed to be among the
bulls-eyes in the dartboard of the capital. I found it frustrating
more than frightening. It hurt me when I used to walk home early
in the morning and see the aftermath of those nightly raids. Piles
of rubble where, only hours before, a home had stood – a family's
nest of peace and security. Worse even than that was watching
distraught people vainly sorting through those ruins to retrieve
something of their belongings. It hurt me dreadfully and I wanted

to hit back. I had been trained by the Army and yet here I was talking into a telephone all night.

I was to play a small part in the downfall of Adolf but I did not realise it even when I was told that, with a few colleagues, I was to be seconded to a top-secret wartime communication post off the Edgeware Road. It was one of the key command units of the great man himself – Winston Churchill.

Our post was in a basement, two floors below ground level. From the outside, the next room looked like a store-room, but it was, in fact, the Strategic Command Room. I had to monitor calls between Churchill and various leading military men in different areas of the war. It might be Montgomery, Eisenhower or Patton – but each one had to be dealt with in a professional and efficient manner. I saw quite a bit of Churchill, he even knew me by name and would often enquire if everything was all right. You had to reply in a direct style and could never try to engage him in unnecessary conversation.

I had made application to the recruiting office in Willesden to be allowed back into the Army so that I could do my bit for King and Country. I knew that my communication work was impor-tant but I felt that my Army training could be put to better use. Eventually King and Country agreed with me and I was back in uniform. I applied to be returned to the 10th Hussars, but they were already in North Africa and so it was decided that the Royal Corps of Signals would benefit both from my Army experience and my communications training.

My first station was Cheltenham, at another nerve centre which is still in use today. Doreen and I took a flat nearby and Doreen even got a job in the local telephone exchange. Once again I found myself pushing and pulling things as a telephone operator and once again I heard the unmistakable voices of Eisenhower and Churchill.

During out of work hours I took full advantage of the wonder-ful sports facilities at Cheltenham. If it wasn't football, it was cricket, running or swimming. I was enjoying myself again. It was all work and all play and, yes! You've guessed it! – I forgot to spend time on my marriage. Doreen found consolation elsewhere and we split. Neither of us fought the inevitable divorce and, before long, we were both free agents, never to meet again. It was a classic case of not knowing the difference between a romance and a commitment to marriage.

It may seem that I am treating the matter very lightly but, at the time, it was very upsetting. However, they do say that every cloud has a silver lining. Well, mine not only had a silver lining but some silver and brass instruments as well. With Doreen departed I found myself with even more time on my hands so, when I heard that the commanding officer had decided to start a company dance band, I was the first to go knocking on his door. I convinced him that I could play both saxophone and clarinet and he gave me some money to go and buy my instruments. I had already seen what I wanted in a shop in Cheltenham and so it was not long before I was back and performing *When The Saints Go Marching In* to prove to the CO that I really could play. He was convinced and before long we had a seven piece band that did the rounds of troop dances, hospital visits and so on. As well as doing my bit on the instruments I began to put in little bits of comedy too – mostly slapstick – and was greatly encouraged by the laughter of the audiences.

There was more encouragement when we played a charity concert at Cheltenham Town Hall on one Sunday evening. Sitting in the audience was that fabulous actor, Rex Harrison, who was touring with a play at the time. At the end of the show he came backstage to say hello. Much to my surprise he singled me out for a personal chat.

"Are you a professional?" he asked me. I replied that I wasn't and he seemed really surprised. "Well," he continued. "If you don't give it a try, you must be utterly mad!"

Those words rang in my ears for a very long time. Rex Harrison had certainly given me something to think about.

Meanwhile, life was as good as could be expected during a

world war. I bought myself a second-hand motorbike which proved to be very special – it had a magic petrol tank that never seemed to run out. No, I didn't have a magic wand or anything like that – but I did know the dark corner where the colonel's staff car was parked up every night. Er...shall we talk about something else?

Socially I was enjoying myself too. I had several girlfriends, especially the lovely Tricia, but having already had a bad experience I was not looking for anything else but friendship and fun. I also continued to play football and several other sports and spent a lot of time knocking about with my best mate, Patrick Dickinson. Our friendship has lasted down to this day.

While I was at Cheltenham I bought another musical instrument – a tenor-sax of my very own. It cost me £12 and it proved to be a great investment. I am still using that American Conn tenor-sax in my act today – more than half a century after buying it!

Cheltenham is a lovely town but my feet were beginning to itch. I wanted to be posted abroad again and made several applications. Finally I was accepted. My CO shook my hand, Tricia kissed me farewell and off I went to the East. Well, Norwich to be precise. I was sent there to an Army transit camp for training before going overseas. I spent a month there and soon crossed swords with a sergeant-major who seemed to enjoy shouting at everyone. I wound him up by pretending to be almost deaf and had him yelling until he turned purple. He finally discovered that I was having him on. He wasn't very happy but he became a little more selective with his shouting from then on.

One day I was hosing down a lorry when, above the noise of the water jetting on to metal, I could hear a lot of shouting. As I went to turn off the water some of the blokes came running round the corner. They were all grinning their heads off.

"It's over! It's over!" they kept shouting.

It took a minute or two for it to sink in. Then I realised that I wouldn't be going abroad after all. The war had ended. Civvie

Street was beckoning again. I knew that I was going to miss the Army – it had provided me with an education, a home, friends, self-discipline and a decent attitude to life. But now... now, there was a new adventure just waiting to be tackled.

"If you don't give it a try, you must be utterly mad!" Those words of Rex Harrison would not go away.

The Army gave us the usual parting gift of a civvie suit, two shirts, a tie and a pair of shoes and then I joined a new army – the battalion of job seekers, thousands of blokes like myself who had not been looking beyond their life in the services and were now at a loose end.

I went back to my mum's place. Her husband, Sydney, was a nice bloke and didn't mind me staying with them. In fact, he was more like a mate and they were certainly happy together, which did my heart good as well. On my first night back at 26 Sherrick Green Road, my mum cooked a shepherd's pie – my favourite – and the three of us sat around the table to share the meal, a bottle of wine and for me a glass of ginger beer. It was just like I had always wanted family life to be. I wished that my brother Fred had been there to complete the scene.

With a full stomach I leaned back in my chair, steeled myself, and then made my big announcement.

"I'm going to try and get into showbusiness!"

I waited for the explosion... for the logic and commonsense to come forth, a sensible argument against Rex Harrison's encouragement. It didn't come. My mum looked straight at me and simply said, "Whatever you think is best dear."

That was it. With the expected protests of my mum not forthcoming, I needed no further encouragement. Rex Harrison and my mum couldn't possibly both be wrong.

That was why, on the very next day, I jumped on a No 93 bus to the Angel, Islington, where the famous Collins Music Hall could be found. It seemed like a good place to start, so me and my demob suit paid it a visit. To me, Collins Music Hall could just as easily have been the London Palladium. When I found myself outside I felt a shiver run up my back, a certain tremble of excitement and apprehension. In the foyer there were photographs of all the big stars – many of whom had started their careers at Collins.

Lew Lake was the manager of the theatre. Anyone who has ever seen an old 1950s 'B' movie which included a scene in the office of a theatre agent or manager can picture what it was like – there was the intoxicating aroma of cigar, alcohol, polish, ink and waste-paper baskets, posters and photos on the wall, and piles of papers on the big scarred desk.

Me and my demob suit were gestured to a chair. Mr Lake asked what I wanted and then sighed when I told him that I wanted to be on the stage.

"Don't be silly," he said, after I had explained to him my experiences in troop concerts and so on. "Do you realise that there are dozens of stars coming out of the forces – established comedians and singers from ENSA, Stars in Battledress and other shows. They are experienced artistes. Go out and get yourself a steady job son!"

My mind went back to the Hippodrome, Cardiff. Was nobody ever going to take me seriously? How could I make people laugh if they wouldn't take me seriously?... if you see what I mean.

As I was leaving, I bumped into a young chap standing at the stage-door looking at a notice-board. He was studying accommodation notices. We started chatting, went for a cup of tea at a cafe across the road and finished up agreeing to share a room. He, Stan, was a musician who had joined the theatre orchestra for a season, and he was able to mark my card on some aspects of showbusiness that I knew nothing about. He was not widely experienced, but he knew a lot more than I did and he was a good companion, as J.B.Priestley might have said.

I did not give up on Mr Lake. I haunted him. Several times a day he would turn round only to find me there – outside the theatre, in his favourite cafe, anywhere! Every now and then I would pluck up enough courage to ask him again if he would give me a chance. His replies became less and less polite. I kept up the pressure for three weeks until one morning as I nodded to him from the next table, as he breakfasted in a greasy spoon cafe near the theatre, he finally gave in.

"All right! If I let you go on first house on Monday and you're no good – will you promise to go away and leave me alone?" The poor man was obviously getting close to hysteria.

I thanked him several times, agreed to the deal and promised that I wouldn't let him down and, more importantly, that he would not regret it.

"I'd better not," he exclaimed, regaining a little of his composure. "If you last a week, I'll pay you five pounds!"

I hadn't thought of that. I was so keen to prove myself that I hadn't even thought of getting paid.

Having tortured Mr Lake into letting me have a go, I thought it was time to start getting my act together. One thing I needed was music for all twelve members of the orchestra. I already had one copy of the things I wanted so I paid one of the musicians a fiver to provide me with another eleven so that Gaucho's Orchestra – that was their name – were fully equipped to back this new 'star' in their midst.

I was thrilled to see my name on the programme, even though it was well hidden among the more spectacular-sounding Lisette Darnier, 'The Atomic Dancer' from the world famous Folies Bergère in Paris, Wendy and Brenda Georgia – 'The Light and Shade of Variety', George Burgess – 'Just a Mug', and Ed Jackson and Dot Brown – 'Doughboy meets Doughgirl'.

Me?... I was billed as 'The Successful Failure' – it was my own idea.

When I arrived at the theatre I was pointed in the direction of my dressing-room, a little area in the cellar. It was a room but, to be honest, I have seen bigger telephone kiosks. There was a mirror and a single light. I would love to be able to tell you that to me it was like paradise – but to be really honest, I was so scared that you could have stuck a pin in me and I

46

would never have noticed because my nerves were already working overtime.

All too soon it was show time. The first house was at 6.15pm and Monday was the quietest day of the week. In showbiz jargon, I had the 'graveyard shift' in the 'quiet house'. In other words I was second on the bill on the Monday early performance.

One advantage of being at Collins Music Hall was that, because of its reputation for new talent, many agents and book-ers would pop in to see that early Monday performance to see if there was anyone worth seeing.

I have been in showbusiness as a professional entertainer for just over fifty years now, and it all began at 6.15 pm on Monday, 17 December 1945. The orchestra struck up and played the overture. The dancers – imaginatively called 'The Girls' – did their stuff and then, all too soon, it was my turn. My mouth was dry, things seemed unreal and it was as if I was watching someone else go through all this. There were about a hundred people dotted around the auditorium and it was my job to warm them up.

"You've got ten minutes, just ten minutes, that's all!" hissed Lew Lake.

Next thing I was walking out on to the stage in a misfit tail suit, trying to appear as much like a classical concert singer as possible. I bowed to the orchestra and then began – *I'll Walk Beside You*, I sang, trying to follow the orchestra as they changed key and tempo with me in their wake. I pleaded with them, got mad with them, and then rushed to the piano on stage to try to show them what I wanted. I tripped, crashed into the piano, slammed the lid on my fingers and so on – and on – and on.

In the wings, the stage manager was hissing at me "Get off!" I was well out of time but I just didn't notice because I could hear the laughter coming from the audience. There was one other small snag – I didn't know how to get off. I knew what I was going to put into my routine – I knew how I was going to start – but I had given absolutely no thought as to how I would finish.

In the end, I just suddenly stopped, said a quick 'goodnight', and ran off.

I got a ticking off from the stage manager and went back to my box. I waited for some sign of approval. Surely someone would give me a thumbs-up? Nobody did. I was left alone with my thoughts. It was a bit of an anticlimax. I felt drained.

Then a thought struck me... I hadn't been sacked! No one had come down to tell me not to bother again. I sat down with a bump.

I was in showbusiness at last.

On The Up

I THOUGHT that, after my first performance, the butterflies in my stomach would cease their fluttering. They didn't!

It was so bad that before the second house I went for a run. When I returned to the theatre I found that the butterflies had returned as well. To cut a long story short, the second show went even better than the first, but still nobody said anything one way or the other.

The same thing happened the next day – and the next. When I look back, I can see how rough my performance really was during those early days, but each of those first audiences seemed to like me. They laughed at all the right times and they were generous with their applause at the end of my act.

Something different did happen after the second show on the third day – I got my first agent! His name was Peters and he introduced himself at my dressing-room door, asking if anyone was representing me. When I replied that there wasn't, he said, "They do now! Could you do Portsmouth Coliseum for a week from next Monday? The pay will be ten quid – OK?"

He disappeared as quickly as he had appeared, leaving his card in my hand. I phoned a few days later and, sure enough, I was on the Portsmouth bill – 'Norman Wisdom, the Successful Failure'.

On the Friday, at Collins, I had another visitor. His name was Martin and he also was an agent. He asked me where I was next week.

"Portsmouth Coliseum!" I replied, rather pleased with myself at being able to say it.

"What about the following week?"

Now at this stage I had better explain that I had already learned, even after such a short time, one of those Golden Rules of Showbusiness – 'if someone talks to you about engagements, NEVER bite their hand off – even if you are desperate!'

Calmly, I took out my 'diary' – actually a small notebook – and thumbed through its pages as if I were trying to find a blank week among my many commitments. At last I reached my decision.

"Yes, I think I could squeeze it in."

"Good!" he said. "You're at the Grand Theatre, Basingstoke, for one week. See you there!"

It did my confidence some good to know that at least a couple of people were interested – but even that didn't stop those butterflies from getting exercise before each show.

All too soon though, the week was over and between the two Saturday performances I was told to go to Mr Lake's office to collect my pay. He counted out five one-pound notes and put them on his desk. Then I had to sign for them. Before I had chance to pick up the notes after signing for them, Lew Lake taught me a harsh lesson. He picked up the cash himself and put it in his pocket. He knew that I had picked up a couple of bookings while I had been working at his theatre.

"Commission Norman!" He said. It was the first time that I had ever seen him smile.

Then he extended his hand, wished me well, and suggested that I might like to appear at his theatre again sometime in the future. I remained polite but I never went back. The lesson? When you're signing for your money, hold it in one hand while your pen is in the other.

The Portsmouth Coliseum was a huge 3,000-seater theatre – a wonderful old place. It frightened me to death when I stood on the stage at band-call and looked out into that vast auditorium. I was in the 'graveyard shift' again – first on after the dancers. I didn't mind that but I was very disappointed when the manager asked me if I would do first-house only since the programme was so full.

"Of course," I said. "I understand the problem." I tried to sound as nonchalant as I could but it hurt inside. It stings a bit when you are reminded that you are a dispensable nobody. Top of the bill that week was a somebody – Teddy Brent – who was a well-known Australian comedian. He was going to teach me another showbiz lesson before the week was over.

I turned up at the theatre every morning at nine o'clock and spent the whole day practising. I would keep on and on until it was time for the audience to be allowed into the theatre. The extra rehearsals certainly helped. My act was getting better as the week wore on. Nobody told me so, I could just feel it.

About halfway through the week, I wandered up to the theatre bar for a lemonade and found several of the cast there, including Teddy Brent. I seized my opportunity and asked him about my act.

"How am I doing Mr Brent? What do you think?"

"You're doing fine Norman," he smiled.

Somewhat reassured, I asked him if he had any advice for me.

"Well, yes Norman," he kindly replied. "You're a visual comedian and I have a good idea for you. If you can get hold of a big iron ball and paint it to look like a balloon, then you can do this little routine with it. You throw it up, head it, catch it, roll it around and trap it with your feet, then you throw it high in the air and let it drop. It will go smashing through the stage and then you can fall into the hole. I promise you, everyone will be screaming with laughter."

As the others rolled about with laughter, I politely thanked him and, after finishing my drink and keeping my dignity, I walked out of the bar. He had really taken the mickey and I didn't need that. However, I had learned another lesson – never ask advice on your act from fellow pros. Since that episode, I never have.

Saturday arrived and this time I did get paid – and there was a bonus when the manager asked if I would play the second house as well as the first.

"Do you really mean it?" I said, unable to contain my excitement. The prospect of playing to a full house on a Saturday night was fantastic. I had already packed, but I was soon back in costume and, this time, I was amazed to find that there were no butterflies. I was buzzing too much to get nervous.

I went on in my usual spot and had the time of my life. This was what it was really all about – there were 3,000 people in the darkness of the auditorium but I could hear every one of them. They laughed at every move and at the end, as I took my bow, soaked in sweat and beaming at them from the spotlight, there was applause such as I had never heard before. I fell in love with every one of them and, even more than that, I suddenly realised that applause was like food and drink to me. It was an expression of people's affection, admiration and appreciation, and to a little lad who had led my kind of life it was the most beautiful sound that I had ever heard.

And so to Basingstoke and yet another new experience. I did my spot in the first half of the first show and then went back to my dressing-room. There was a knock at the door and the manager appeared. At the sight of him I began to expect the 'first house only' request, but instead he said, "You were very good Norman! I was wondering if you would go on again in the second half and do another spot?"

Bloomin' right I would! There was just one problem though – I didn't have a second spot.

I never have let small details like that get in the way, however, and my mind went into overdrive as I frantically tried to decide what I was going to do. I had less than an hour to work something out. The manager was still waiting in the doorway for my reply. I began to realise that my first reaction had been a little hasty. Finally I spoke,

"I'll tell you what," I said, hoping that I wasn't going to lose my chance. "I'll be honest and tell you that I haven't got the material ready to go on again today... but I will by tomorrow!"

I held my breath. A second-half spot is a big leap in prestige and I dearly wanted it. I also knew that if I let my heart rule my head I would probably mess it up and do myself more harm than good.

"All right, that'll be fine! Thanks Norman," said the boss and he hurried away. I remained frozen to my chair until the door had closed... and then I danced all round the room.

I never got to bed that night. I sat up and changed my routine to develop the work with the piano a bit more by adding more bits of visual comedy. Then I brought in some other instruments which I had left back in London – my lovely tenor-sax and a piccolo. I felt that by making these changes and additions I would have enough material for two different spots.

It was dawn by the time I had settled for my new departure and then I had to make yet another departure – for London in order to get my instruments. I slept on the train, dashed to my mum's house for the instruments and caught the next train back to Basingstoke. I didn't sleep on the way back because I was repeatedly going through the new routines in my mind.

By early afternoon I was back in the theatre and practising to an empty auditorium. You may have seen some of my piano routine, but in those days it was a little different. The spot started with the curtain rising to reveal me leaning on the piano reading a newspaper while eating a sandwich. When I realised what had happened I would go into panic overdrive, shove the crumpled newspaper into my pocket and hide the sandwich under the lid of the piano. My hand would be trapped by the lid and from then on it became utter chaos. I would try to sing my way out of trouble but finished up having trouble from the orchestra. All the other instruments came into play later with more comedy and then some straight numbers to finish.

It was soon show time and that meant now or never. I went through both routines exactly as planned – and the audience howled. I felt great, especially when the manager came round, shook my hand and gave me a twenty-five per cent pay rise. I was now on £12 10s a week (all right twelve pounds, fifty pence if you insist!)

Even better, I had a visitor – Mike Sullivan – who was putting a touring revue together for Will Hammer, a quite well-known impresario. It was to be called *New Names Make News!* I was offered two spots, a part in a sketch... and £15 per week. Did I accept? Not 'arf!

Our first stop was the Grand Theatre in Blackburn. I was not the only comic on the show, there was also the very experienced George Francis, whose speciality was monologues. In the sketch we worked together, in fact I was his feed or, if you prefer, his straight man!

The course of life never runs smoothly and, if I had known what was going to happen at Blackburn, I might never have gone there. As it happens I am glad that I did. The first show was a little low-key. I did my stuff and there was polite applause, but where was all the laughter – the richest sound in the world? I soon found out. The manager came to the dressing-room and he didn't mince his words.

"They don't like that sort of thing here! You'll have to do something different for the next house – or else!"

I couldn't believe what I was hearing. Everything had been going so well in recent weeks and now here I was on the receiving end of some pretty harsh words. My mouth went suddenly dry and I felt a lump in my throat.

"Or else what?" I asked quietly.

"You'll be out!" He came back bluntly.

He waited. I didn't know what to say. Finally I blurted out, "I can't! I just can't!"

"Oh well, I'm sorry but there it is!" he said, and walked out.

I was devastated and close to tears. All that work and now this. I felt as if my world had just caved in.

This just wouldn't do. I had to pull myself together. I couldn't just give up. An inner strength welled up inside me. Suddenly I was that street urchin once again, stealing fruit to quell my hunger pangs. I leaped out of the room and chased after the manager. He was already in his office before I caught up with him. I knocked and waited for him to call me in. He seemed surprised to see me.

"I've come to apologise and explain," I said. "You see, I'm really a singer but I wanted to try and make people laugh."

"Well obviously you can't!" he replied. "Just get out there and sing – stick to what you know!"

I thanked him for the reprieve and flew back to the dressing-room where I dug deep into my cases to find some music that I'd collected. There were two numbers – *They Didn't Believe Me* and *Some Other Time*. I only had music for one person so I then had to work my way out of the problem with the orchestra. I solved it by asking the pianist to come up on stage and play the grand piano that I had used for the comedy. The next problem came when I realised that my usual second-half spot came just before the final act – a singer!

It was too late to do anything about it so I just took the plunge. There was quite a splash as I sang my two songs. The applause was terrific. As I walked off the stage the manager stopped me and said, "That's much better. Why didn't you do that in the first house? Take a tip from me – forget about the comedy, stick to your singing!"

To put the icing on the cake, an agent had been watching and he booked me to appear at the Pavilion, Hastings, a few weeks later – as a singer!

The singer who followed me at Blackburn was furious, but I succeeded in keeping out of everyone's way and saw the week out. At the end of our time there, George Francis had a chat with me in one of our quieter moments.

"I want you to know something Norman. One day you're going to be a big star – and that day isn't too far away. I want you to have this…"

With that he gave me a silver-topped walking stick. It was one that he used in his act. I tried to refuse it but he insisted, saying, "It will remind you of your early days Norman!"

He was right. I still have it. That walking stick has pride of place at my home on the Isle of Man. I often pick it up and hold it for a few moments, reliving Blackburn and the wonderful encouragement of the lovely George Francis.

The tour continued and I was getting used to life on the road. Most of the time we all stayed in the same digs at each town we visited and, as always when showbiz folk get together, the stories came thick and fast. It was lovely to listen to the experiences of everyone else, and it is still one of my favourite pastimes. I learned a lot and I laughed a lot.

At the end of each theatre run we all piled into a coach to go to the next town. The journeys were always exciting for me because we were passing through and stopping at towns that I had never seen before. My early travels had taken me to India and South America, but I had never before sampled the delights of places like Burnley and Glasgow.

Glasgow!... Yes, I've been there!... The dreaded Glasgow Empire!

It was never really dreaded as much as it was made out to be. It was nicknamed 'The Cockney Comic's Graveyard' – but this was mainly due to the fact that Glaswegians are not really in tune with the London accent and therefore patter comics suffered simply because they could not be understood.

The Glaswegians would encourage them by shouting things like, "That's nae funny! Gi'e us somethin' tae laugh at!"

I nearly succumbed to this myself. In the first house there was a stony silence to greet my patter and something between a snigger and a yawn resulted my visual work. I quickly concluded that the second house offering would have to be a bit different. It was different all right. I did the whole thing without saying a single word – I mimed everything, added a few extra sight gags – and won them over. I got a great reception at the end and I shall always be grateful to the great Glaswegians. Thanks to them I had to add another dimension to my act – one that has been of great benefit to me ever since. Thanks Glasgow!

Remember that booking that I got as a singer? Well, when I finished the tour I went to the Hastings Pavilion and appeared as engaged. No, I didn't stay as a singer. In the first house I went on and sang *Some Other Time*. Once I had done that I went into my comedy routine. After taking my bow I went straight to my dressing-room and waited. Sure enough, not many minutes went past before there was a knock at the door and it was flung open.

"Hey, that was smashing!" said the same agent who had booked me. "You could almost be a comedian!"

It would be nice to be able to tell you that a star had been born and that we all lived happily ever after. I'm afraid that life isn't like that though, is it? It is very nice and very flattering when an agent comes to your door and offers work – but don't believe that it's always like that. Far from it! Most entertainers in their early days spend hours scanning through the pages of *The Stage and Television Today*, which is the profession's weekly newspaper. They constantly scour through the 'Artistes Wanted' column, hoping to find that one job that will give them a break – and lead them on to success and stardom.

I was no different. I had my out-of-work times, and even in those days *The Stage* was compulsory reading. Seeing the advert and applying for it was no guarantee of getting the job either. Times don't really change much. In every walk of life there seems to be more people chasing fewer opportunities. I searched and I applied constantly, but without too much success.

My earnings were not too bad so I was able to pay my way while I stayed at my mum's. After Hastings I scanned *The Stage*, but there was not much doing. I didn't despair though, I was filling in time before my next engagement – my very first pantomime. I was already booked into *Robinson Crusoe* at the Grand Theatre, Brighton – and that was an exciting prospect.

Even if I had not had the engagement with the panto to look

forward to, I would still have been looking at *The Stage*. I had been an errand-boy, I had been a ship's boy, an Army lad and a telephone operator. I was extremely grateful for all of these experiences – they had all taught me something about life and myself, and they had certainly supplied me with food in my stomach and a roof over my head.

There was no way that I could go back to that sort of existence, however. My course through life was set. I had rubbed shoulders with showbusiness people, I had stood under the spotlight, I had felt those butterflies that turned you upside down before you stepped out into that spotlight and, most of all, I had felt that wave of affection which washes over you when you hear the laughter and that most wonderful, wonderful sound – the applause of an audience!

Yes, my course through life was set all right. I was stage-struck – and on the up!

Oh Yes I Can!

I LOVE Pantomimes! They are like no other kind of show. There is always a special atmosphere from the audience, and to work in a panto is real fun. It can be hard work, of course, much harder than a variety show, but it is always so very rewarding – and I don't mean financially. I think that pantos are special to me because so many family groups go to see them. You become a part of the experience that the family enjoy together and then you are forever a part of that family. These lovely shows have that mood of unity, togetherness and happiness that it is impossible not to enjoy them.

There is almost always a similar spirit of goodwill among the cast as well. Everyone becomes affected by that family feeling and there is a much more light-hearted atmosphere than usual behind the scenes. There always seems to be a few parties, too, and so it becomes like one family group entertaining lots of other family groups.

I have appeared in many pantomimes but I have to say that there is nothing like your first one. My first, as I have already mentioned, was at the Brighton Grand for the winter season of 1946-47. I had no panto experience whatsoever but, by the time the run was finished, I felt that I had been appearing in them all my life. Renee Houston was Principal Boy – Billy Crusoe, Hugh Rene was Mrs Crusoe, Olive Lucas was Robinson Crusoe, Jean Carson played Polly Perkins and Donald Stewart was, if I remember correctly, good old Man Friday. Me?... I was the Mate!

It was a wonderful show and my colleagues in the cast really did make a mate of me, helping me through this special new experience. I received my highest fee so far for that show – £25 per week. That was good money compared with what the hard-working 'man in the street' was able to earn. But there was much more to it than the money. It was a marvellous time for me. I worked my routines and acted my part as well – perhaps the first stepping stone toward the comedy actor that I was later to become.

The icing on that particular cake came in the shape of my very first real newspaper review. There had been various mentions before, but only as listings. The *Brighton Gazette*, however, did me proud. I still have that press cutting among my many souvenirs. I have always treasured it and, if the critic who wrote it is still alive today, I'd just like to say thanks very much. It said something like this: 'Every pantomime needs a really good comedian and *Robinson Crusoe* is lucky to have just such a mirth-maker in Norman Wisdom, whose versatile antics stole the show.'

I hope my mentioning it does not make me sound big-headed. It's just that I was really pleased and proud when I saw it – and when I look at it now I'm able to relive that moment in my life. I'll tell you something else too – my mum was pleased as well when she saw it.

The only thing that it didn't do was to have agents camping on my doorstep, eager to make me a star. I didn't really expect that it would, but I was always an optimist. Sometimes optimism can get stretched to breaking point and that was what almost happened to me when, for the first few months of 1947, there was nothing in my diary. I was not too concerned at the time, but it did help to keep my feet firmly on the ground.

While I continued to look for more work I stayed at my mum's place once more. I bought a sparkling new AJS motorbike, which cost me £35. I had always loved motorbikes, and I still do. I decided that I could afford this one so I went for it and it gave me much more freedom of movement.

Among the various places in which I sought work was the famous Windmill Theatre. Vivian Van Damm had advertised for acts and so I went along for an audition. I had only done a few minutes of my act when he waved me aside and called "Next!". He did thank me for attending but that was it – I was a failure, and not a successful one either. There was another young man auditioning on that same day and he was given a booking. Today he is well-known throughout the land but, in those days, no one had ever heard of the man who was to become Sir Harry Secombe.

He was a nice chap even then and he commiserated with me in my failure.

"Never mind mate, you'll make it!" he said. We often see each other now and have a laugh about that first meeting. That was the only time I ever went to the Windmill Theatre. I never even went back to see the show – honest!

In between seeking work, I enjoyed riding around on my motorbike and, one day, decided to take off for Kent. It was just on the off-chance of seeing some of the people I used to know – including, perhaps, my brother Fred, whom I had not seen for about sixteen years. My mum had lost touch with him as well and could only tell me that the last she had heard of him he was working for a coal-merchant along the Kent coast. That had been before the war so anything could have happened since then.

I thought that I would start my sleuthing at Deal, where Hawksfields were the local coal merchants. If Fred was still in the same line of work they might be able to give me a clue. It was not so easy to remember where Hawksfields' yard was when I finally arrived in Deal, and so I stopped to get my bearings. A bloke was walking toward me down the road so I decided to ask him instead of charging off in all directions. Knowing my luck, I thought, he would probably turn out to be a visitor to the town and have no more idea than I had. Have you ever noticed how often that seems to happen?

"Excuse me, do you know where Hawksfields' coal-yard is?" I asked.

"Yes mate! It's just around the…" The bloke stopped talking with his mouth open.

He stared at me and seemed unable to continue. I've got used to being stared at like that now, but it was a bit disconcerting then. He finally seemed to find his voice.

"Norm?"

Suddenly it was my turn to stare in disbelief.

"Fred?" I croaked. "Is it really you Fred?"

Sure enough it was – next minute there we were, hugging each other and jigging about on the pavement as if we were demented. We must have looked a right couple of twerps to anyone passing by, but we didn't care.

It was great to see him and he immediately took me home to meet his wife, Christine. What a reunion! I told him my tale and he told me his. I was really proud of him because he had a beautiful home and a lovely wife. He also had an excellent job as area manager of a top coal firm which put him in charge of the whole of South-East England. I also discovered that I was not the only sportsman in the family. Fred had taken to rowing and had won the South Coast sculling championship.

We vowed never to lose touch again and we never did. My brother was my best mate when we were kids and, although we had lost touch for so long, my affection for him had never diminished. I was thrilled to bits that we were in touch again. Mum was delighted too – we were a family again.

At long last my months of inactivity were brought to an end in the shape of a letter from promoter and agent, Bert Montague. He had seen me in the pantomime at Brighton and, as soon as he knew that he was going to put out a variety tour, he got in touch with me. It was a good offer too. His revue, *Let's Make Hay!* was for fifteen weeks and I was to receive £45 per week. Bert also became my agent and so when that letter dropped through my door it was quite a red-letter day for me – in fact, much more than I realised at the time.

I could hardly believe that I was going to earn that sort of money and I celebrated by buying my first-ever car – a lovely green 1937 Morgan, which could really shift. All right, it's confession time! I am a complete car and motorbike nut and I will travel miles to visit particular showrooms but, in those days, much of the appeal in owning a car was because it would attract the attention of the fairer sex. Well, I wasn't exactly tall, dark and handsome was I? I had to get noticed somehow!

The new show was great. I shared a dressing-room with another comic, Charlie Cameron. He had a lovely assistant, Freda Simpson, who was also one of the dancers. She used to visit the dressing-room a lot because of her work with Charlie and the three of us hit it off from the very first day of rehearsals in a church hall in Acton, in West London. I think I fell in love with Freda right from the start and, no matter how much time I spent with her, I wanted more.

One Saturday morning we took off in my car for Bournemouth and met her parents. I didn't want the day to end. Freda's parents were very nice. It could not have been easy for them to have their daughter suddenly appear on their doorstep with this little nutcase driving a green, open-top Morgan. I remembered to stick my little finger in the air when we had a cup of tea and, as we chatted away, I think that they were actually starting to like me.

The following Monday, still in rehearsals, the show's director, Hastings Mann, took me to one side. He had a look in his eye which seemed to me to mean trouble. I was completely wrong.

"How would you like to do a special charity show, Norman?" He asked.

I didn't hesitate.

"Yes, of course," I replied, thinking that he meant in a few months time.

"Good! It's this Sunday at eight o'clock!"

I gulped.

"Where is it?" I squeaked.

"Er, I'll tell you on Friday," he said, and quickly changed the subject.

There was some big mystery here. I tried not to think about it. I concentrated on the rehearsals for the tour and also made up my mind as to what I should do in the charity show. I guessed that I might be short on time because there were certain to be other acts, like myself, willing to give up their Sunday evening.

At last, on Friday, I was able to confront Hastings Mann again. Finally, he told me the whole story. Another comic had got laryngitis and I was to replace him. It was a Water Rats charity show – at the Victoria Palace! No wonder he had kept it from me. The Victoria Palace was one of the most prestigious venues in the business. It had been a kind gesture on his part because he had not wanted me to worry about it.

So now, I was faced with the prospect of appearing at THE Victoria Palace for the Water Rats – the leaders of entertainment. WOW! And there was even more to come! Hastings confessed that he had also held back on a little more information which might have caused me some sleepless nights. Among the other artistes on the charity show programme were Clarkson Rose, Charlie Chester, Will Fyffe, Harry Tate Jnr, Nat Jackley and Vera Lynn – some of the biggest names in the business. Oh yes, and another thing, top of the bill were a couple of comics called Laurel and Hardy... Laurel and Hardy!

I still get an attack of nerves just remembering how I felt when all this was divulged to me.

On the day of the show I was directed to my dressing-room – way up in the roof, backstage. For those not familiar with how it works, the higher your status, the nearer to the stage is your dressing-room. Mine was the furthest away on that particular occasion. After I had dumped my gear in my room, I wandered down to the stage where a few of the big names were chatting and running through their requirements.

Will Fyffe and Charlie Chester both spoke very briefly, but that was all. It was not that people were impolite, it was just that showbusiness folk tend to stick together – and if a stranger wanders in he tends to be ignored if he is not recognised. It is as much a form of shyness as anything else.

I ran through my routine and actually heared a little applause from the auditorium. It was dark and I could not see who it was that was encouraging me at that time.

Just before the show was due to start, Vera Lynn's pianist approached me.

"Mr Wisdom, we're sorry to ask you this at such short notice, but Vera has asked if you would change places with her. She has to catch a train immediately after her spot and she's a bit worried that she might miss it. Would that be okay with you?"

All it meant was that I would go on one place later in the second half, so I did not have a problem with that. It gave me the chance to stand in the wings and watch her perform. She was wonderful. The audience were totally enchanted by her. They joined in with *We'll Meet Again* and *The White Cliffs of Dover*, and gave her a standing ovation as she hurried from the stage.

They were still applauding when I burst on to the scene. I was caught up in that magical performance too and worked myself into the floorboards to please that lovely audience. I went a storm. I had never before experienced anything quite like it. They stood, they clapped, they cheered, and I was sent back by the stage manager to take four curtain calls.

When I finally came off the stage I was grabbed and given a big kiss by – none other than Vera Lynn!

"Hang on a minute," I said. "I thought you had a train to catch?"

She laughed and explained. "I'm sorry about that – but I saw you perform at Brighton and I thought that you deserved a better place on the programme. I knew it would be a big opportunity for you, and I knew that the audience would love you – so I thought I would be your warm-up instead of the other way about."

I didn't know what to say. What a pro! It was a wonderful gesture that did so much for me and it is one that I have never really been able to repay. Vera – You are the tops!

After the show there were many agents knocking on my door and I was kind of pleased to be able to say that I already had an agent. They all gave me their cards, though, and I was very happy that they did, because one of them was to play a major part in my career a little later on.

I hardly slept that night because I was still on a high from the excitement of it all. Nevertheless, it was straight back to work the next day with the *Let's Make Hay!* tour. It was a good show and was received well. Bert Montague had put together a neat package with an international flavour. It went a little awry, though, when the American trio, Forsyth, Seaman and Farrell, had to return home after the first month to fulfil other engagements. It was already arranged that they would be replaced by a Canadian act, Alfred and Elsie Price, who arrived in time for the show's opening in Manchester.

This couple led to me having a rather unpleasant experience. It came about because, even after a few days, it was obvious that they were becoming increasingly annoyed at how well I was going down with the audiences. From the moment that they had arrived they went around telling everyone how good they were, while the rest of us just got on with our own work and chatted about the things that people normally chat about.

In the business, being professional means a lot more than just being paid for what you do. Unprofessional conduct was a cardinal sin – it still is, although I believe that the standards have sadly slipped – as they have in most walks of life. Well, Alfred Price committed a terrible act of unprofessionalism when, after a few days of joining the show, he walked on in my act and started making comments to the audience about what I was doing. Even with my limited experience I couldn't believe what was happening.

After I came off, I went straight to the Prices' dressing-room to speak to Alfred.

"Please don't do that in my act again, you're ruining it!" I said, as politely as I could.

"I'm the star and I'll do whatever I like, whenever I like!" replied Alfred.

I decided to let it rest and hope that it wouldn't happen again. But it did! He was quite cunning because he did not do it at every performance. I appealed to the tour manager, George Hollis, but it was quite obvious that he had quickly become bosom pals with Alfred and Elsie Price. He just shrugged his shoulders at my appeal.

"There's nothing I can do! They are the stars of the show and they can do what they like. I can't do anything about it!"

I let it drop yet again. It happened several times more through the tour.

The last night of a tour is always something a bit special. There's the sadness at parting from friends and also the determination to go out with a bang. Our last night was at the famous Metropole Theatre in Edgeware Road, a prime venue and one of those theatres that everyone likes to say that they've appeared at.

Between the last two performances I went round to the Price's dressing-room to clear the air and say that there were no hard feelings on my part. Elsie looked at me and simply said, "Push off you little creep!"

Alfred was not far behind. "You heard what the lady said – get out!"

I was disappointed but I left without pursuing the matter. I had learned another lesson – being top of the bill is one thing, being a star is something entirely different.

No, that was not the end of it. In the very last show he did it again. This time though, after he had walked on in my act and said, "Hey, it's funny! — it's really funny! You'll split your sides!", I mimicked his walk off as if it were a part of the act. When we got into the wings I landed one of the sweetest right hooks to his jaw that I have ever thrown. Down he went — out for the count. I breezed back on to the stage and continued with my act without further interruption. The audience never knew anything about it.

George Hollis was in the wings when I finished. He caught hold of my lapels and red-faced he stormed at me, "This is the last time you'll ever work in this theatre! In fact, I'll do my best to make sure that you never work again!"

I was past caring by this time so I slammed another right-hander into him. He shot backwards and collapsed amid tumbling scenery and props. Perhaps I had just blown my career — but I went out like a lion, and I felt all the better for having expressed myself in the only way that these particular people seemed to understand.

At the end of the tour I had just two dates in my diary. The first was a one-off show in a holiday camp at Skegness. The second was a much bigger engagement at which I was just beneath star billing. The star was Freda! Yes, we got married at a Methodist church at Shirley, near Croydon, on 7 October 1947.

She looked a picture in pale blue and I couldn't believe my luck in that she had agreed to marry me. I felt as if Buttons had actually won the hand of Cinderella. We had a great ten-day honeymoon in Brighton and I was very, very happy. I now had a lovely wife and my career seemed to be going in the right direction.

Life had often told me that I would never make anything of myself, but I felt that in some way I had responded to the challenge in true panto tradition — "Oh yes I can!"

The Gump

WORK seemed to dry up for a while after we were married. I didn't break my neck looking for any and neither did my agent, Bert. Gradually it began to dawn upon me that maybe I should be looking for a new agent rather than for a new job. Before I was able to set about doing just that, Bert came up with a cracker of a booking. It was in a new show entitled *Piccadilly Nights*. I was to be the show's principal comedian at a salary of £50 per week – and there was a place for Freda. That was really good news because the show was to appear at the Alhambra in Brussels! Yes, we were off to good old Belgium.

What about the language problem, do I hear you say?

Well, I am very proud to tell you that I am multi-lingual… I can trip over a piano in any language that you care to name!

I learned, parrot-fashion, how to introduce myself in French, which seemed to be the best option, and, as the bulk of my work was visual, there was not too much else to worry about. We were booked for two weeks and it turned out to be quite an experience. On the downside, we were never paid and so we had our two weeks living costs plus our travelling expenses all to come out of our own pockets. But on the up side was a real silver lining because, topping the bill were none other than Laurel and Hardy, who actually remembered me from our charity show at the Victoria Palace.

We chatted a great deal during that couple of weeks and Stan remained a friend until he died in 1965. We very nearly worked together during that engagement. I was involved in a slapstick routine based on wall-papering and, one night, my partner couldn't make it to the show because of illness. Stan immediately offered to fill in but the manager told him that he couldn't because of a clause in his contract. If it had not been for those few written words I might have been able to tell you about Laurel and Wisdom.

The Laurel and Hardy films made these two wonderful people real legends and it was a great thrill for me to be able to get to know them. People have a habit these days that, if someone is quite good at something they are often referred to as a 'genius'. It must be one of the most over-used words in the English language. Where Laurel and Hardy are concerned, however, I would use that word to its fullest extent. They were not only brilliant at what they did but they were also such nice people. I don't ever remember seeing either one of them ignoring anyone, refusing to sign an autograph or to have a chat, and they were always so polite to everyone that they met. They were true professionals, very down to earth and thoroughly nice guys who retained a humble attitude in everything that they did. They were my kind of people. No airs and graces. They were just there to make people happy. What stars!

Work was still very scarce and I was beginning to get concerned. I continued to practise every day and once startled a window-cleaner who had just reached the top of his ladder and peered through my window just as I was going through a face-pulling routine. He was so shocked that he fell off his ladder, fortunately landing unhurt, and ran off up the road leaving all his gear behind. It was a good thing that my mother knew him and was able to phone him and explain. The poor window-cleaner was still in a state of shock and said that he wasn't sure if he was being threatened by a lunatic or some sort of ape.

My mum had actually moved to Deal by this time and kept a room there for Freda and myself to visit, even though we now had our own flat in Willesden. We spent a lot of time in Deal and I was able to show Freda all my old haunts as well as having many happy get-togethers with my mum, Fred and his family.

Family get-togethers and practice were all very fine but I was beginning to wonder what was happening to my career. Was this it? Had I gone as far as I could go? Surely that wasn't true. I was getting nowhere with Bert – that was becoming increasingly obvious – but where else was I to go? I remembered all those business cards that I had been given by agents and I began to sort them out. One name seemed to nudge at me more than all the others – Billy Marsh.

In those days Billy Marsh was with London Management, one of the top agencies in showbusiness. Their office was in Jermyn Street, not far from Piccadilly. I decided to take a chance and go along to see him. When I was shown into his office he recognised me straight away. Billy was a small man, always very neat, very alert, usually with a cigarette on the go and always with a sense of humour. He was very sharp and astute. Before I could drop any hints as to what I wanted, he asked me what the problem was.

"I can't seem to get any work," I blurted out. "I'm with Bert Montague but there doesn't seem to be much happening."

Billy Marsh took it all in his stride as if he had been across this same territory many times before.

"There's only one way to settle this," said Billy. "We'll have to go and have a chat with Bert!"

We went, there and then, and Billy and Bert talked while I sat there like a bag of sugar that two people were haggling over. The upshot was that I now had two agents who would split the commission whichever one of them got me an engagement. That evening I talked for hours with Billy Marsh, swapping stories and discussing my future. By the time I left I was happier and much more optimistic than I had been for some time.

A week passed and still nothing happened. I had to remind myself of how positive Billy Marsh had been. It wasn't that I was losing faith – but I was beginning to wonder. At last – ten days after our first meeting – Billy Marsh phoned me.

"Hello Norman, I've got a job for you at Brighton Hippodrome, taking the place of A.J.Powers who has had to pull out because of illness. It'll be a good booking for you because the Hippodrome is owned by the Moss Empire chain and will open their eyes to you. What do you say?"

I didn't need asking twice.

"When do I start?"

"Tonight!"

"Tonight?" That one word hit me like a bullet.

"Yes... Can you do it?" Billy sounded impatient.

"Well, yes!" There was no doubt in my mind. Within an hour I was on my way to Brighton. When I got to the Hippodrome I was met by some very familiar words.

"You're on in the first half – after the dancers!"

It was the 'graveyard shift' again. I didn't mind. I was just happy to have the chance to get in front of an audience again – any audience would have done!

The first house went well and the manager came to see me after the show.

"Thanks for filling in. You went so well that I'd like to put you on in the second half for the rest of the week."

The theatre was packed for the evening performance and I went on in the second half as arranged. The applause was deafening. It felt wonderful and it earned me another little bonus from the manager.

"That was terrific!" he said. "I've just phoned Val Parnell and told him that he's just got to come and see you!"

For those who don't know already, Val Parnell was like the Emperor of China – the very top man in the administration of British showbusiness. I was flattered that the enthusiastic manager should think that I was fit to be in the same town as Val Parnell, let alone that he should come especially to see me perform.

The following night the theatre was filling up nicely and I was just getting changed for my act when the manager came round to see me yet again.

"He's out there!" He informed me.

"Who is?" I asked.

"Val Parnell! Third row, aisle seat. Give it all you've got!"

Well, once I'd been to the loo again, I composed myself and tried to keep the butterflies perched until my big moment. I was much happier once I finally got on stage. Again the audience was marvellous. They laughed and they clapped and they cheered. I took my bow and went back to my dressing-room.

I had not been there many minutes when a message instructed me to go to the manager's office. When I got there, Val Parnell was in the room. He smiled and asked me to sit down. He waited just long enough to light up an enormous cigar and then spoke, quite quietly.

"Mr Wisdom, I'd like to make you a star! I think that you have something."

I almost lost my voice but I managed to gulp and croak, "Oh, Thank you very much sir!"

"I shall put you on at the London Palladium," he went on. "I shall also want you to sign on with an agent of my choosing."

I knew that somewhere there was bound to be a snag. I know that I had been with Billy Marsh for less than a fortnight but I just couldn't brush him aside as easily as that.

"I don't think that I can do that sir," I croaked. "You see, if it hadn't been for Billy Marsh I wouldn't have been working here tonight and you might not have seen me anyway."

He was unmoved. "That is the way of showbusiness Mr Wisdom!"

Perhaps it was the way of showbusiness, but it was not the way of Norman Wisdom and, as politely as I could, I said as much to Val Parnell.

"Very well Mr Wisdom," Val Parnell extended his hand. "I shall be going away for a week's holiday. Think about it while I'm away and let me know when I come back."

We parted on those amicable terms and I immediately phoned Billy Marsh. The next day he travelled down to see me. He listened to what had happened, watched the show and then phoned Bernard Delfont, who was Val Parnell's main rival. Parnell had the Palladium, Delfont had the London Casino, another big status venue in the capital.

Somehow or other, Bernard Delfont arrived at the Brighton Hippodrome in time to see my act in the second half of that evening performance. He left again immediately afterward. I didn't know what to think. All my bewilderment ended, however, when Billy Marsh came into my room, grabbed my hand and began shaking it furiously.

"Well done Norman!... You're on – the London Casino!"

Much later, I learned that the story of my loyalty to Billy had meant a great deal to the Delfont Organisation, which was run by the Grade brothers, Leslie, Lew and Bernie. They had a firm belief in family loyalty – and that included members of the showbusiness family too.

Whatever the reason I was now booked for a major West End venue for the first time. Once again my billing was 'The Successful Failure' although, in the programme, I was labelled 'The New British Comedian'. It was an exciting show and I didn't get the 'graveyard shift'. Top of the bill was Allan Jones, an international star in his own right in those days, but perhaps better known today as father of the great Jack Jones. Also on the show were the legendary Wilson, Kepple and Betty – Harrison and Fisher, a dance act from America – trick cyclist Marie Wilson – the Six Elwardos, a troupe of acrobats – Maurice Rocco, the Boogie-Woogie pianist-dancer – BBC comedians Bennett and Williams – George Doonan – the Casino Girls and Harold Collins Casino Orchestra.

I still had much to learn and my education was furthered when I turned up for rehearsals and found that my spot was to run for only eight minutes. It was the musical director, Harold Collins, who told me and it took me by surprise because my act usually ran for fourteen minutes. In the stalls I could just make out the figure of Bernard Delfont. We had not met before but I recognised him. When I got the opportunity I slipped away from everyone else on stage and sat behind him in the darkened auditorium.

"Excuse me sir…" I began

"Welcome to the West End, Norman," he interrupted with a warm smile.

"Thank you very much sir," I pressed on. "There's just one little problem, I've been cut to eight minutes sir!"

"No Norman, I'm sorry but it's going to have to be six minutes. We've got such a crowded programme."

"But my act runs for fourteen minutes – I can't cut it down to less than half!"

"I'm afraid you're going to have to Norman! That's the way it is!" He remained friendly but I could see that there was no chance of any sort of compromise.

Now I was faced with a real dilemma. I had the cheek to just go out there and do my full act anyway, hoping that it would go down well enough for them not to sack me on the spot. On the other hand, I could do as I was told, cut down to six minutes and struggle to make it half as good.

I decided to take the risk and I assured Harold Collins that the music would be the same and I would cut down on my other work.

Well, the moment finally arrived. It was Monday, 5 April 1948. The butterflies were working overtime. Before I knew it I was in the wings waiting to go on. Maurice Rocco came off and assured me that it was a good audience. I went on and did my stuff. I really went for it in a big way. Nothing was left out. I could hear the laughter and that spurred me on. I did the full fourteen minutes but I was actually on stage longer than that because the audience wouldn't let me go. They were wonderful and gave me three curtain calls.

My grin of delight melted away instantly when I saw Bernard

Delfont waiting in the wings. The applause was still ringing around the auditorium but I knew that I was for the high jump. Rules were rules. I hadn't just bent them a bit. I had broken them into pieces. There was no avoiding Mr Delfont so I went straight up to him to take my medicine.

"Well done Norman!" He said, and shook my hand so vigorously that he made my teeth chatter. Then he walked away to watch the rest of the show. There was no reprimand, no reminder about doing only six minutes. Nothing!

The second house was soon underway and I did my full fourteen minutes again. Once again the audience roared and once again I got away with it.

As was often the case in the West End, everyone waited around at the theatre until the early editions of the daily papers arrived. We all wanted to see how the critics had reviewed the show. When they arrived I was stunned. According to the papers I had stolen the show.

I went home but had not been there for very long when a knock came at the door. It was David Lewin from the *Daily Express*. He wanted to interview me and had brought a photographer with him. The result was an immediate feature in the following day's newspaper – some of which went like this:

WISDOM'S THE NAME...
He woke to find that he had joined the star comics
Portrait of a comedian. Norman Wisdom, who woke yesterday after a first-night appearance at the London Casino and found himself named as a new star.
"I don't believe it," he said. "I've still a lot to learn".
Wisdom, aged 27, married, living at Willesden Green, London, began entertaining when he was in the Army. He found that he could get laughs by clowning. He had no need to tell jokes.
His face is mobile, can be twisted into any shape. He tumbles on to the stage, shadow-boxes, tries to play the

piano, pulls out a clarinet, tires of it and turns his attention to... a great, vast sandwich. Then he pleads with the audience to follow him in an Eastern song – in Gibberish!

His props? A stringy tie, an old shirt and a baggy evening suit several sizes too large.

The West End gave this ex-shop assistant his big break. "I hope I shall come back later", he said last night, "and show I deserved it."

Suddenly my name was being mentioned to the millions who read the national newspapers.

The rest of the company were great about all my publicity. There was no hint of jealousy, only congratulations. Even when everyone else had to lose a little time to accommodate my full routine, still nobody moaned. I felt especially bad about Marie Wilson, whose spot was cut from six minutes to ninety seconds. I was on my way to speak to the manager about it when she stopped me.

"No Norman, it's all right – honestly. You see, I don't mind at all. Nobody knows this yet but I'm pregnant and doing the shorter time suits me fine. I'm still getting the same money so you've actually done me a favour."

I was moved to the second half of the programme which is a kind of promotion and I went well again the next day and the day after. If there was any danger that I might start to feel a bit too important, it was soon put into perspective. After the second show on the second day there was a crowd of fans outside the stage-door. They were all waving their autograph books in the air. I took the first one and was just about to sign it when its owner said, "Oi! What do you think you're doing?"

"I'm signing your autograph book!"

"No you're not! We're waiting for Allan Jones!"

I slunk away quickly, before my face went too red.

Two days in the West End and never a dull moment. I awoke

on the third day to an even more dramatic piece of news. Billy Marsh phoned me.

"Norman, are you sitting down? I think you'd better before I tell you my piece of news."

"What's the matter?" I had all sorts of things running through my mind.

"Allan Jones has got laryngitis! Bernard Delfont has made you top of the bill!"

I should have been sitting down because I nearly fell down when he told me that. Top of the bill!... Me! The Successful Failure!... Norman Wisdom from Paddington, Deal, Buenos Aires, Lucknow and Willesden. I couldn't believe it.

Never again would I be anything less than top of the bill. From that day on Wednesday, 17 April 1948, until today, that has been my position. Allan Jones never returned to the show and I remained in the prime position for the rest of the London Casino season, which finally ended on 1 May 1948. Straight away I was booked into the Golders Green Hippodrome as the star of the show.

The offers were now flooding into Billy Marsh's office. I was earning £100 per week, which was good money in those post-war years. We continued to live in Willesden and there was no immediate change in our lifestyle. I suppose that I was being cautious because I couldn't really believe that all this was happening to me. I was still the errand-boy at Lipton's who nobody was really bothered about.

I sat in Billy's office to discuss where I was going next and he showed me all the terrific offers he had received. Even while I was sitting there the telephone never stopped ringing. But I was worried. It was all happening too rapidly for me now and I didn't honestly think that I was up to it... not yet!

"What on earth are you talking about? Look at all this lot!" Demanded Billy, holding up a bunch of papers.

"I know!" I tried to explain my mixed feelings. "Don't think, for a minute, that I don't appreciate all that you're doing for me.

You're getting me top jobs and good money. You've made all the difference in the world to me. It's not you – it's me! I need more time to get together what I can call a real act. I want new sketches, comedy routines, singing, dancing, the lot. I don't know how, just yet, but I want to build up a character that is completely unique. It's all right, at the moment, being the 'new British comedian', but that can't go on for ever. I need to be able to build up something different."

Billy didn't argue. He thought about it for a moment.

"Well Norman, you're the one doing the act so, fair enough, if that's what you want! Now, there is one show here that you might fancy. It will mean a drastic drop in your money though. It's a lengthy summer season at the Spa Theatre in Scarborough, but they're only offering £35 per week. You'll be working with other acts if you want – and it might give you the chance to try out some new stuff. The show is called *Out of the Blue* and this will be its third season. Do you fancy it?"

I didn't hesitate and I couldn't wait to get there. Freda and I bought a caravan, which was an adventure all of its own. The very first time that I drove it, the coupling came loose and the caravan overtook the car! As you may imagine, our eventual journey to Scarborough was not without its hazards. We didn't make it in one day and had to spend one night on the side of the road. Any experienced caravanner would have gone into hysterics if they had seen my attempts at levelling the trailer. Our home on wheels was so lop-sided that we couldn't even boil a kettle without holding it in place on the stove.

When we finally got to Scarborough, I was helped to set the caravan properly and our home for the next three months was in a lovely spot overlooking the sea. Freda and I were very happy and cosy in our little home and became so used to it that we even had friends from the show come back for a bite to eat after the performances.

The show itself was, indeed, an education. The programme had to be changed regularly so that the holidaymakers would be encouraged to come and see us more than once. It meant that we continually had to create new material, which was exactly what I wanted.

Quite by accident, Scarborough proved to be yet another milestone for me. I was sharing a dressing-room with a conjuror. Just like me he was having to produce new material and he didn't find it easy. Then he had this brainwave.

"Norman, how about if I ask for a volunteer from the audience, you come up and we fool around for a bit. It might get a few laughs. What do you think?"

Always eager, I nodded.

"Fine! Let's see how it goes. I'll go and get myself a different suit and we'll see what happens."

I hunted around Scarborough but couldn't quite find what I was looking for. Not that I really knew what I was looking for... but I knew it would click when I finally saw it. Eventually, I wandered down a little side street and glanced into the window of a second-hand shop. At the back of the shop I could see a rack of clothes and so I went in to look.

It was in that little back-street shop that the Gump was born! The Gump is the name that many people have given to my character. The word actually means lunatic, idiot or, if you prefer, berk! It's an apt description of me both in and out of character, don't you think?

In that shop I found a scruffy checked suit. I tried it on and it was a bit small – even for me – but it felt right. I walked up and down a bit in the shop and it felt as if I'd always been wearing that suit. Then I spotted a checked cap that matched. The two together were just the job. The suit was thirty bob – sorry, shillings! Okay then, one pound and fifty pence. The cap cost me an extra shilling.

I have since had thirty-five Gump suits made but that was the very first, and I still have it – another great memory-jerker that shares my home in the Isle of Man.

Come showtime and the conjuror calls for a volunteer. I

strutted up on to the stage and we went into a totally unre-hearsed ad-lib routine that brought the house down. It went so well that within two days we received a flying visit from Bernard Delfont who had travelled all the way up to Yorkshire just to see our routine. He immediately booked us both into the London Casino to repeat our success.

The conjuror? He was David Nixon, who later became a household name in his own right. He has since died and is still sadly missed. Anyone who ever met him will tell you that you could never have met a nicer man. It was an honour and a very great pleasure to have worked with him and become friends. A little tear still comes to my eye when I remember that he is no longer with us.

We had a marvellous season at Scarborough. It was hard work but it gave me exactly what I wanted, and the routine with David developed nicely. I used to strut on to the stage, shyly at first and then with growing confidence. He used to show me tricks that I thought were wonderful and then, when he was demonstrating what he wanted me to do, I would end up doing the trick. He would humour me, get annoyed, control himself, get exasperated and finally give up – just as the trick went right.

The audiences loved it. The 1948 version of *Out of the Blue* was a great show and the Spa Theatre was packed all the time.

As well as new material, I had made quite a discovery in the Gump. I found that the audience was more sorry for me in this new character than they had been in the past in the character of the down-trodden little man in the out-size suit. I began to play it up, laying on the pathos to see how far it would stretch. Sometimes I overdid it, getting laughs where I hadn't intended. Through it all a new character was slowly emerging and this one was much more clear-cut than any I had ever attempted before.

At the end of that summer season we were on our way back to the London Casino. Freda and I parked our caravan at Hendon and the Casino season got under way. David's role changed a little in that he became my straightman in our routine rather than me being his comedy sidekick.

It was a great month back at the London Casino, hugely successful and a lot of fun. David and I could have developed our double-act but, although we were firm friends, we both wanted to pursue our own individual careers and so resisted the temptation.

David's simple idea at Scarborough had certainly given me a new dimension to my work – that elusive ingredient for which I had been searching. As a conjuror's assistant, I had created the character that was to become my trademark – The Gump had been born!

On The Telly

AFTER the success of *Out of the Blue* and at the London Casino, the world was fast becoming my oyster. That's a daft expression really because oysters make a lot of people ill! But you know what I mean. In 1948 things had taken off in a big way. Few people, including myself, realised that this was still only the start.

At the end of the year I was in panto again at the Alexandra Theatre, Birmingham, in a role specially created for me – Norman Crusoe! I had been promoted from Mate, you see. Seasons aren't the same as they used to be. Few theatres these days keep a panto for twelve weeks, but that was fairly common in the 1940s, '50s and even into the '60s.

Of course the panto was *Robinson Crusoe*, but Norman was Robinson's long-lost brother – as if Robinson wasn't lost enough already. You can do anything with a panto script and there was plenty of space to accommodate my routines. The *Birmingham Mail*, the local evening newspaper, was kind and gave me a nice write-up which said something like: 'This quaint and highly original comedian sets his signature on his part, endears it to us, and makes it peculiarly his own.'

I never knew that I was 'quaint' or even 'peculiar'!

"Are you sure that you didn't write this yourself?" demanded Eddie Leslie. Now Eddie was the Dame – and a Dame good one too! Not for him the Danny La Rue style. He had the build of an England rugby international and made no secret of the fact that he was a clown in Dame's clothing. We became immediate pals, and Eddie was to play a part in the further development of Norman the Gump.

The panto, with Betty Huntley-Wright as the hero, was a huge success and was booked for a repeat season at the Grand Theatre, Wolverhampton. It is quite usual for pantos to do the rounds if they are a proven winner, but it is not so usual to be booked in at a theatre so close to the one that they have just been to.

Following the Birmingham panto, I was back on the road again. Billy Marsh was keeping me on my toes with week-stands at many of the country's top theatres – Swindon Empire, Bolton Grand, Folkestone Pleasure Gardens and York Empire to name but a few. I was certainly clocking up the miles and getting a complete education in the geography of Great Britain.

On the down side I had my first real failure. It was not my fault but, if you are involved with something that flops, you can't help but take it personally. I was excited when entrepreneur, Cecil Landau, booked me for his Cambridge Theatre revue, *Sauce Piquant*. Being in a West End revue was always something to write home about. Also in the show were Tommy Cooper, Douglas Byng, Moira Lister, Peter Glover, Muriel Smith and Bob Monkhouse.

There were dancers too. Among them was a young lady that you may have heard about – Audrey Hepburn!

John Fernald was the show's director. He later became top man at RADA but, with all due respect, I don't think that this revue was entirely his thing. It was a very full programme – too full. I had enough time to do my stuff but the performance was rather 'bitty', with nobody really having the time to 'feel' the audience. I was not allowed to use my Gump suit either. It seemed that, in the West End, I had to be rather posh and wear a tailcoat. I didn't really mind the tailcoat but it did mean that I had to adjust my character.

Anyway, the show went down like the *Titanic*. Even from this catastrophe there was a silver lining or two. I was supposed to do a dance routine with Audrey but, as she was a good five inches taller than me, it wasn't so much a Fred and Ginger as a David and Goliath! It just didn't work. When we were told that it was being dropped from the show, the lovely Audrey kept apologising to me through her tears.

"Hey, dry your eyes! It's not your fault," I said. "Don't let it get you down. These things happen in this business. I'll tell you what – you've got what it takes and you're going to be a big star one day! I know it, you know it and you have to make sure that everyone else knows it too. Never lose faith in yourself!"

"Do you really mean that Norman?" Audrey stopped crying.

"I wouldn't say it if I didn't!" I replied. "Now it's up to you to get out there and show 'em what you can do."

The press reviews after the opening night were not exactly impressive, but they did pick out just one person for special praise. No, it wasn't me – it was the lovely Audrey Hepburn! That particular cloud had a golden lining for her since she never looked back from that moment. A star had certainly been born.

The other silver-lining for me was sharing a dressing-room with the late, great, Tommy Cooper. What a character! Tommy was six feet four inches tall and he made me feel like a midget. He had an amazing sense of humour and you never knew what he was going to do next. Some days he was so incredibly dry that you really thought he was being serious – that is, until he had suckered you in long enough for the pay-off line! Other days he was totally slap-stick with his humour.

He loved to wind people up. There is the famous story of him getting a taxi and when the cab arrived at its destination he paid the driver. Then he reached in his pocket and said, "Oh – and here's a little something for a cup of tea!" The happy driver would hold out his hand for the expected tip and Tommy would give him a tea-bag.

That was the hilarious Tommy Cooper – and he was never any different all the time that I knew him. A complete nutcase – but one of the most lovable people that you could ever wish to meet.

Bob Monkhouse was also on the bill at the Cambridge Theatre, as I've already mentioned. In that particular show Bob did not do his own spot but took part in various sketches which also involved Douglas Byng and myself. Even in those days it was obvious that Bob was going places. He was a smart young man, quick-witted, fast-talking, very professional and well-mannered. You couldn't help but like him.

Since those days he has become a household name in his own right and is, by far, our best television host. He is slick, witty and every bit the professional that he set out to be. Bob is a very interesting man to talk to. He has an amazing knowledge of films, especially the old comedies, he is a great raconteur, a very talented cartoonist and, of course, he is a very creative script-writer. Add to all this his acting ability and his immense skill as a stand-up comic and you have one of the greatest assets in British entertainment.

When you see Bob with game-show contestants, making quick-fire responses to their remarks, don't think that it has all been rehearsed over and over again. Bob doesn't need to – he has one of the best brains in the business.

Oh yes, there was one other memorable moment from *Sauce Piquant!* It was on opening night. We were all on stage to take a final bow and, as the applause rang out, I could hear a woman's voice yelling, "Norman Wisdom, Norman Wisdom!" I waved in the voice's general direction, but the sound persisted: "Norman Wisdom! Congratulations, Norman Wisdom!"

At last we left the stage and returned to our dressing-rooms. Tommy and I were changing when a call came through from the stage-door manager.

"There's a lady to see you Mr Wisdom!"

"Send her through!" I was really keen to meet this lady who had been so eager to make her presence heard.

A few minutes later there was a knock at the door. When I opened it, there was the lady – my mum!

"Could you hear me Norman? I was so proud of you, I just had to let you know!"

That's mums all over isn't it?

The theatre work continued, as it does down to the present day, but more of that later. In the late 1940s there was a new 'stage' which could be viewed by many more people than could be accommodated in even the largest of our theatres. Television! It was not a new invention, but it was becoming more and more available to the average household. At first, every street had at least one home with with a television and, whenever there was any sort of major event, like the Cup Final, everyone around would be invited to pop in and watch.

Later, of course, most homes in Britain had a television set, right up to today, when there seems to be a television in every room. Television now rules the household! It is the altar in front of which families gather to perform that sacred ritual – balancing a meal on a tray – on a knee – on the floor! It is the babysitter, the escape from reality, the informer, the persuader, the salesman, the teacher, the companion, the shopping mall, the conscience-easer, the politician – the BOSS! But in those days it was the infant – there to be humoured by being looked at for an hour or two if time allowed. That infant has finally become a time-consuming monster!

My very first television appearance was on Saturday, 22 November 1947 at 3pm. I was an also-ran in a show with the imaginative title of *Variety*. It went out live and gave me my first experience in front of the cameras.

The show went out from the Alexandra Palace. Joy Nicholls introduced it – remember her? She was a lovely lady, really nice. The rest of the show included comedian Frank Raymond, soprano Gwen Catley, conjuror Dennis Forbes and a gospel choir called the Southern Singers. I had six minutes to fill and it was a great baptism for me because it was live. You went on and did your stuff without a lot of fuss. There was no stopping and starting, or anything like that, as you get with today's recorded shows. For me, it was just like going on stage and doing my spot, except that I had to watch that I didn't crash into the cameras when I was throwing myself about.

As I said, it was a great experience – and I even got paid! Yes, my fee was £15! BBC fees don't change much!

Just under a year later, I was on the box again. It was on 18 October 1948, and the show was called *Wit and Wisdom*. Yes, my very own show. The *Radio Times* even gave me a mention. Me! – in the *Radio Times*! Even the Lord Mayor of London only gets in there once a year!

'New Comedian – his props consist of no more than a comic baggy dress-suit, an old shirt and stringy tie, and his clarinet.' They didn't waste words in the *Radio Times*!

The show was a forty-five minute spectacular – well, it was forty-five minutes anyway. I was back at the Alexandra Palace with the BBC's resident 'group' – Eric Robinson and Orchestra. My special guests were Dorothy Squires and Billy Reid. *Wit and Wisdom* went on air at 3pm and we did a repeat performance at 8.30pm two nights later.

There was another *Wit and Wisdom* in August 1950. They probably couldn't believe the first one. Before that, on 8 July 1950, I was in another TV show called *Music Hall*. It was not long after the *Sauce Piquant* disaster and I really needed something to cheer me up. *Music Hall* did the trick and I soon had a spring in my step again – that's what you get for keeping your shoes under the bed! Both *Music Hall* and the second *Wit and Wisdom* were directed by Richard Afton and they proved to be by no means the last time that we would be working together.

My television work must have been OK because I even got a mention in *The Observer*. I was rubbing shoulders with Lords,

Ladies, Bishops and Barristers in that paper. *The Observer* said – ahem – 'Television has discovered a clown so prodigally endowed with talent that he might become another Grock if someone will take him in hand.'

Cor Blimey!

Now someone once told me that if I really wanted to make it, I would have to go to America. Hollywood, Broadway – those were the places where the real superstars hung out. I listened, of course, and finally decided that it was time for Norman Whittington to tie his knotted handkerchief to a stick, sling it over his shoulder and set off to where the showbusiness streets were all paved with gold.

I invested my savings and flew to New York. I was extremely excited. It was not just the travelling but the prospect of taking my career to new heights, and the possibility of meeting all the big names of this wonderful world of showbusiness – great!

When, at last, I arrived in new York – the Big Apple as they call it now – I found a cheap room in what passed for a hotel, just off Broadway. On my first evening I went for a walk through those world-famous streets of theatreland – that giant stage upon which huge stars, such as Gene Kelly, glittered for their fans. It was marvellous!

Imagine a child making his first visit to a Santa's grotto or to Disneyland, and you have me on Broadway. The lights, the queues, the theatres, the big names, the excitement – the entire kaleidoscope of glittering entertainment! It was wonderful – absolutely wonderful. I saw Broadway much as a fan would do, and yet I also felt strangely at home. I was a part of this magical world of fun, spectacle and illusion. Perhaps I was still little Norm from the Deal Sea Scouts but, like everyone else on those super-stages of Broadway – I had my dreams and I was following them!

Ed Sullivan was presenting a TV show called *Toast of the Town* – an extravaganza which featured international variety acts. That's the one for me, I thought and the very next morning

I did a bit of detective work and found the number for his agent. I introduced myself, got a curt reply and had the phone put down on me... So I did a bit more detective work and found out where Ed Sullivan lived.

It was about eleven o'clock in the morning when I rolled up at the Delmonica Hotel on Park Avenue. Ed Sullivan had a luxury suite there, on the ninth floor. I gave my shoes one last polish on the back of my trouser-legs and walked up to the hotel receptionist.

I really put on the English officer's accent, and said, "Good morning! Mr Sullivan please... I have an appointment!"

The receptionist immediately stood to attention, gave me the floor number and told me that it was Suite 901. So far so good. As I approached Suite 901, the familiar butterflies let me know that they had flown all the way from England just to be with me in my hour of need. It was really nice of them, wasn't it?

A servant soon answered the door after I had pressed the bell.

"I have an appointment with Mr Sullivan! I'm Mr Norman Wisdom from England!"

I couldn't believe that it was that simple. He politely asked me to follow him – no, he didn't say, "Walk this way!" – so I did just that, I followed him. The next thing that I knew, I was shaking hands with Ed Sullivan. He was still in his dressing-gown and he looked decidedly puzzled.

"Mr Wisdom, you'll have to excuse me but I don't seem to remember..." he began, as politely as he could.

"It's all right Mr Sullivan! It's me who should be apologising for cheating my way in here like this. I just had to see you... I want to be on your show!"

For a moment he seemed quite stunned by my revelation but, in the end, with folded arms, asked, "What exactly do you do?"

I didn't need asking a second time.

"I'm an English comedian. I saw your show and I'd just like a chance." I didn't pause for breath, grabbing every second while I was still there.

He sat down, relaxed with his hands behind his head, and said simply, "Okay! Show me!"

I went into my routine and did about four minutes before he stopped me.

"I'm sorry but that's just not the sort of stuff I use on my show. I do wish you well though – and I want you to know that I admire your initiative."

We shook hands and I thanked him for his time.

"There's something I'd like you to know too, Mr Sullivan," I said. "I appreciate you not having me thrown out... you're a real gentleman!"

I left and went into a crowded bar near my 'hotel'. Perhaps I'll get spotted here, I thought, after all it is near Broadway. So, completely off the cuff, I found a space in the middle of this huge packed bar and started to do my stuff. At first just one or two people glanced over their shoulders at me but then, gradually, one by one they all turned away and completely ignored me! Didn't they know that I was Norman Wisdom from England?... .No! They didn't! To them I was just another New York nutter.

I took the next plane back to England.

It was good to be home and I had a panto back at the Alexandra, Birmingham, to look forward to. This time it was *Cinderella* and I was to be Buttons, my favourite panto role. Betty Leslie-Smith was Cinders, Helene Cooney was Prince Charming, Ruthene Le Clerc was Dandini, Betty Nelson the Fairy Queen, Michael Moore was Baron Hardup, Terry Kendall and Nick Nelson were the Ugly Sisters, and also in the show was that great harmonica act, The Three Monarchs. They could really play and were very funny as well. Oliver Gordon was the panto director.

The panto was another success and, during the run, I was visited by Henry Hall, who wanted me to appear in his summer show, *Buttons and Bows*, which was due for a long summer season at the Blackpool Grand. Donald Peers was on the show and he was a big favourite with a lovely voice. The only problem was that I also sang and I thought that maybe that might have been a problem.

Henry Hall was a very experienced gentleman – and I do mean 'gentleman'. He was lovely. He refused to be ruffled by anything. His word was his bond and he never had a bad word to say about anybody. His orchestra, also, played beautifully. It was no wonder that he was so popular.

"Don't worry Norman! I assure you that you will be able to sing," he said, as we shook hands. So I went to Blackpool and did my stuff – including the song *They Didn't Believe Me*, which I particularly liked and had used in my act as a straight number for some time.

Donald Peers watched me on opening night and then came round to my dressing-room. He was a man of few words. He didn't knock. He just marched in and said, "Cut out the singing!" Then he marched out again, slamming the door to underline his order.

I didn't cut it out of course, and so he went to Henry Hall and complained, using the threat that he would quit the show. Henry sent for me, explained the situation, and said, "I hate this kind of bickering Norman, it is all so unnecessary. I gave you my word that you could sing Norman and I'm keeping my word!"

Donald Peers didn't believe it! He thought that as he was the star nobody would dare to cross him. Within two weeks he was gone, to be replaced by one of Blackpool's all-time favourites, the brilliant George Formby.

Working with George was marvellous. He was a great, great entertainer who was loved by everyone. His films had been box-office record-breakers and, on stage, he was one of those performers who could receive a standing ovation just for being there. Many times I used to stand in the wings and experience the sheer magic of George and his ukelele.

By the way, there was a stage-hand at the Blackpool Grand called Pete. I don't remember his surname – in fact, I probably never knew it – the hard-working backstage people always seem to be known only by their first names. Anyway, Pete saw me in my battered, tight-fitting suit and said, "Hey Norm, I like the Gump suit!" That was the first time that I had heard anybody use that word. So, although the character was born in Scarborough, he was finally made official in Blackpool. Well done Pete!

The summer season was great. Some entertainers don't like to be in one place for too long because they like new challenges and new horizons all the time. I am a bit like that myself, but it is still nice when you can get a bit of time to yourself and a long summer season can often give more opportunity for that. It's not that the only thing to do is turn up at the theatre just before show-time, perform and then go away again. Personally, I have always liked to practise a lot because that is what keeps you on your toes. There are also press and public relations commitments – interviews, judging beauty and baby contests, taking part in the carnival and all that sort of thing. That summer in Blackpool had all those ingredients – and I enjoyed every minute of it.

I told you earlier that Henry Hall had visited me to arrange the Blackpool season while I was in panto in Birmingham. Well, he came more than once and on one occasion he brought with him his pal, Claude Langdon, who was also a major impresario. Claude wanted to know if I could ice-skate.

"Can I ice-skate? Can I ice-skate?" I replied, with all the indignation of an Olympic gold-medalist. I didn't actually say that I could – after all, I'd never been on the ice in my entire life, had I?

We made arrangements to meet again six weeks later at the Empress Hall in London where I would be able to show what I could do. No sooner had they departed than I was fixing up my first skating lessons.

When the appointed time came round, I journeyed to Fulham, swaggered up to the Empress Hall and met Messrs Hall and Langdon. We were the only people in that huge building – like three peas in a bath-tub. I put on my new skates and explained that I would probably be a bit rusty.

"Never mind Norman, we understand!" said Claude, and then they watched me perform as if I had been born with skates instead of feet. I was hoping that I wouldn't fall because, under my clothes, I was more black and blue than the average ink pens. Learning to skate had been a painful experience.

I got the job and appeared in a show called *London Melody*. It was a really big production with a much bigger cast than I had previously experienced. Although I had star billing, the star of the show was really Belita, an English-born ice-skating actress who had made a number of films in Hollywood. The show had a plot – just! Like most ice spectaculars, though, the story-line was very flexible and had characters ranging from Napoleon to a cockney waiter called Angelo. I was that cockney waiter. It was another bit of déjà vu for me! I got to sing with the fantastic Empress Hall Orchestra, conducted by Harry Rabinowitz, and I was having the time of my life.

There was one disaster with the show when it was in rehearsal. We had a gorilla chase sequence in which this chap in a skin would appear among the girders about 150 feet up in the roof, grab a rope and slide down it, then chase me round the ice while the chorus girls all fled shrieking. During one rehearsal he missed the rope and plunged 150 feet on to the ice. He died instantly. It was awful and it still sends a shudder through me when I think about it.

On opening night the place was packed – which meant that there were ten thousand people in the seats. Gracie Fields was among the audience and led the applause at the end when we all took our final bow on the stage at the rear of the ice. Belita had organised the finale line-up and put herself at the front with me behind the chorus line – all five feet, five inches of me!

Henry Hall walked on and took the microphone. He congratulated the cast, thanked the audience and welcomed the special guest, Gracie Fields. The audience wanted her to sing, and she did indeed cross the ice and step on to the stage. Instead of singing, she unexpectedly pushed through the chorus line, grabbed hold of little Norm by the hand, and led me to the front of the stage.

She gave me a little kiss and said, in her broad Rochdale accent, "In a coople o' years, this lad's goin' t'be the biggest comedian in Britain!"

It brought the place down. Henry asked me to walk her back across the ice to her seat and, on the way, I thanked her for what she had done.

"Don't worry lad, I'm an old professional. I could see what was going on and I couldn't let that happen to you!"

Toward the end of that run at the Empress Hall, I had a special phone call from Billy Marsh. We were on the phone to each other all the time of course, but this one was rather special because it was a summons. No! Not a court summons – something much more exciting.

"Get over to Lew Grade's office! He wants to see you straight away!" said Billy.

If Lew Grade wanted to see you, then you sprinted all the way. There was never a problem in finding his office – you just followed the smell of expensive cigar. Before long I found myself slumped in a big chair with about an acre of shiny desk between me and the great man.

"I saw you in the show last week Norman! It was great and so were you. I had a friend of mine from America with me. He's quite well-known over there and he wants you on his TV show. Sullivan's his name… Ed Sullivan! How about it?"

I didn't give the game away. I was excited of course – but I kept calm.

"Great!" I replied. "Just tell Ed that I'll do it for two thousand pounds!"

"WHAT!" Lew Grade nearly chewed through his cigar. "Two thousand pounds! Are you crazy?"

"Just tell him that If he agrees then I'll do it. If not – forget it!"

I didn't really feel that cocky inside. I had my fingers, toes and everything else crossed – well, almost everything!

Lew phoned through to the States while I sat there. He was even more amazed when Ed Sullivan agreed.

"You've got it!" He gasped.

I smiled. Lew didn't know the full story and I knew that Ed Sullivan couldn't possibly have recognised me – or even remembered me – from that brief encounter in his hotel suite.

The reason that I had asked for so much money was that I wanted Billy Marsh to come with me – and I wanted enough cash for us to make the most of the trip.

I had not given up on my idea of breaking into the American scene and I thought that, if anyone could pull it off for me, then Billy Marsh was the man to do it.

So, there I was, heading back to the USA to make my debut on big-time television.

Top: The St Luke's
School team –
Guess who's
holding the ball?

Bottom left: How I
looked as a trainee
waiter at the
Artillery Mansions
Hotel. Posh eh!

Bottom right: A 14-
year-old man about
town. I might have
scared Al Capone!

Left: The bugle boy.

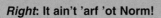

Right: It ain't 'arf 'ot Norm!

Below: The brass monkeys – that's me on the left.

Left: Wisdom of the 10th Hussars.

Right: Boxing clever in the Army.

Below: In the Royal Corps of Signals dance band – 1943.

'COS I'M A FOOL

Left: This is how I looked at the start – Collins Music Hall, 1945.

Above: 'The Thinker' – Wisdom style, 1946.

Left: My first TV appearance – anything for a laugh!

Norman Wisdom – The Gump, Esq.

Left: Marjorie Jones as Miss Medworthy, telling me off in *Fine Goings On* on the wireless.

Left: Look – no hands! A 1953 practice session.

Below: The 1954 *Sinbad* programme.

Above: Sharing a joke with Princess Margaret after she saw *Sinbad*.

Left: With Pip Hinton in *Where's Charley?*

'COS I'M A FOOL

Above: Giving Sugar Ray Robinson some boxing lessons.

Below: My second meeting with Joan Crawford – in Hollywood.

Above: The Navy lark in 1934. I borrowed the gear from a Navy lad just for the photo.

Above: Blowing out the candelabra with Liberace. The cake was from the Variety Club of Great Britain.

Left: With the lovely Vivien Leigh.

Above: Getting to grips with Schnozzle Durante.

Left: 'Big-hearted' Arthur Askey.

Left: Laurel and Hardy and Wisdom.

Up in the world – in Piccadilly.

'COS I'M A FOOL

Right: The Norman Wisdom show at Wimbledon Theatre in 1975.

Below: My mate Bob Hope.

Left: **My wonderful agent, Billy Marsh.**

Below: **Dear old pals – George Formby and Roy Castle.**

A hug with Gracie Fields.

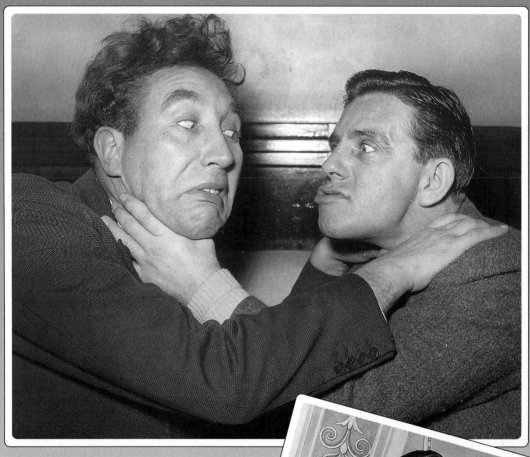

Above: Getting it in the neck from Frankie Howerd.

Right: I might be old-fashioned but I'm not a millionaire, Eartha Kitt.

Right: Sammy Davies Jnr visited during the 1965 shooting of *There Was A Crooked Man*.

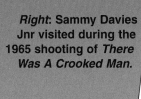

Above: "Sign here!" says Val Parnell.

Right: Being humoured by the great Jerry Desmonde.

How The West Was Won!

SO THERE we were, two intrepid explorers, two pioneers hitting the trail to conquer the Wild and Woolly West. The Pilgrim Fathers on the *Mayflower* would have been proud of us.

Okay – let's be honest. There we were, Norman Wisdom and Billy Marsh, sat on an aeroplane and crossing the Atlantic in comfort – waited on hand and foot by lovely stewardesses. Actually, even that is not quite right. The surroundings were as I have described and, certainly, Norman Wisdom was there... but, alongside him, was this shivering wreck of a man who could only just answer to the name of Billy Marsh. Billy was petrified of flying and it was only the regular application of high-powered alcohol that kept him from total and utter collapse. Poor Billy had been reduced to jelly from when we got to within ten miles of the airport.

Our journey across the Atlantic to the US did nothing to help Billy overcome his fears. I noticed a sudden increase in activity among the crew, but I didn't actually think anything about it until

I happened to glance out of a window. I couldn't believe my eyes! There were flames playing around one of the engines. Most people were dozing – but I wasn't. I caught the eye of one of the stewardesses but she signalled me to keep quiet so as not to cause a panic. Too late – I was already panicking!

A few minutes later and the captain announced that we would be diverting to Reykjavik for an emergency landing. Billy sobered up in a flash – and there was no sign of a hangover. He buried his face in a pillow and prepared to meet his Maker. As it happens, the captain and his crew were absolutely magnificent. They landed the aircraft with the minimum of anxiety to the passengers and the emergency services tackled the blaze instantly. All was well except that we had to wait a full seventeen hours in Iceland before another plane was available to take us on to New York.

By the time that we finally landed in America I felt ready to take on everything that was likely to be thrown at me. Billy was already worrying about the return flight.

That Sunday night I was on the *Ed Sullivan Show*. I did my normal sort of act, ending with my one-band – which was rather like a maniac band-leader trying to play everything himself. The studio audience thought it was great and I understand that there was a similar feed-back from the viewers.

After the broadcast, Ed Sullivan chatted to me as if we were old pals. He was still totally unaware that we had met before.

"Great show Norman – well done!"

I couldn't stand the suspense any longer. I had to say something.

"You don't remember me do you?" I asked with a grin.

His blank face showed me that he didn't, so I decided to put him out of his misery.

"I'm the bloke who came to your hotel and did an audition – you told me that you didn't have that sort of thing on your show."

Suddenly the penny dropped. His perplexed look changed to one of recognition.

"So it is!" He grabbed me and gave me a massive hug. "Well, how about that? I never realised! Well done! Well done!" He was even more excited than I was.

That was not the last time that I appeared on the *Ed Sullivan Show*, but that occasion, just for the sheer expression on his face, was by far the most memorable.

We had not finished with the States yet, not by any means! Back at the hotel after the show there was a message waiting from Paramount Pictures, asking if we would go to their offices the following morning to arrange a screen test.

Our appointment was for 11am and we arrived five minutes early. After we had waited until 11.15, Billy suddenly stood up and said, "Right! That's it! We're off!"

I couldn't believe it.

"They've got to think that we're important," said Billy. "They're not going to keep us hanging around like this! Trust me Norman."

I did trust him, of course, but I was beginning to think that the plane experience had finally sent him a bit barmy.

"I'll lay a bet with you that, by the time we get back to the hotel, there will be another message waiting for us, asking us to go back."

He was quite right, naturally. Billy phoned them immediately, played hard to get and then arranged for us to go back to Paramount the following Thursday. We had a week in the States and planned to make the most of it.

By the time our appointment came around we were ready for them. There were three Paramount executives ready for us too. We met in the boardroom like some scene from *High Noon*, except that none of us were carrying guns. They wanted us to go to Hollywood for screen tests almost immediately and offered air tickets and accommodation. Billy accepted the accommodation, but said that we would rather travel by rail in order to see more of the country. You can guess why!

Our train journey was aboard a first-class sleeper and Billy was happy – or rather, Billy was happy for a while! On the way we encountered workmen clearing away debris from the tracks. Debris that was obviously from a major train crash! Once again, Billy reached for his 'medicine'!

Our accommodation was the famous Beverley Wiltshire Hotel, frequented by the rich and famous. A chauffeur-driven Cadillac was put at our disposal and yet Billy was not at all happy. He didn't like the way things were shaping up. On the surface we were being treated like royalty, it's true, but Billy's instincts were telling him something else. From my point of view we were being treated like big-time movie stars. Our suite was fantastic and, after we had checked in, a message came in to say that a car would be sent for us at 11am the following morning.

Since we had a day to play with, I was up for a bit of star-spotting – but Billy had other ideas. He dragged me along to a photographic studio, hired a model and had the photographer take pictures of her and me together. He wanted instant copies which he then took to a press agency. Next day all the newspapers in Britain had a picture of Norman with a young lady in Hollywood. Billy had done it again!

Paramount Studios flung open their gates to us the next morning and we were soon in yet another executive office. John Littlejohn was the man who we were seeing. What a farce! He thought that Billy was Norman Wisdom and that I was his manager. Our host was more than a little embarrassed and apologised profusely for his error. He went on to explain that the project in mind was a film called *Pleasure Island*. As we left he asked, "You won't hold the mistake against us will you?"

Hardly realising what I was saying, I replied, "Of course not! Definitely not! No, no, no."

In the meantime, Billy's mind went into overdrive again and later, when we returned to England, I was front-page news in the daily papers again – 'Norman says "No" to Hollywood!'

The interview at Paramount fizzled to nothing and we put it out of our minds as soon as we left the studios.

We still had time to kill before our flight home and now it was my turn to put it to good use. There was one international star that I really wanted to meet and I had heard that he was currently in Hollywood, directing a film at his own studios. Billy tried to contact him for me, but without success and he was forced to give up. For once, it was the guile of Norman the street urchin that won the day.

I phoned the Fillmore Studios and asked to speak to him. I was asked who I was.

"It's Norman Wisdom! I'm a British comic and I'm on a visit from England to do the *Ed Sullivan Show*. I wondered if I might speak to him?"

Nothing happened for a moment or two and then a different voice came on to the line.

"Hello! Charles Chaplin speaking."

Yes, I had done it! I had got through to my hero – Charlie Chaplin. I was thrilled to bits. I could hardly speak and just garbled back, "This is er... Norman Wisdom, Mr Chaplin... I, er... that is... I wondered... well, I know you're busy but er..."

Charlie put me at my ease.

"You may be a little surprised to know, Mr Wisdom, that I *have* heard of you. Why don't you drop by this afternoon. It would be nice to meet you."

Wow! I had no hesitation in agreeing. Just fancy that! The great Charlie Chaplin had actually heard of me! Little Norm had come to his notice! I could not believe it and now I was actually going to meet him! Wow! Wow! Wow!

We went straight after lunch and were shown to the studio where he was directing Claire Bloom in *Limelight*. Two typical studio chairs were provided and we were able to watch him at work for a while. Then he came and sat with us and we chatted for almost an hour and a half. Before we parted company I asked if he would do his famous walk for me.

"We'll walk together," he said. "I'll do my walk for you – but you must do your walk for me!"

We did exactly that and, for me, it was a piece of sheer magic. He added a touch of gold as well when he quietly whispered to me, "Young man, one day you will be following in my footsteps!"

I told nobody about those few lovely words. Nobody else had heard them and I didn't want to share them. After all, who was likely to believe me anyway? A few years later, however, he repeated them himself in a newspaper interview.

"Norman Wisdom is the comedian who will follow in my footsteps!"

I still have that press cutting to prove it.

It was praise indeed from a real comic genius. I had laughed at Charlie Chaplin for years and I cannot tell you how much of a thrill it was to have that meeting with him. It was one of the greatest experiences of my life. My mum was thrilled to bits when I told her – after all, not many mums can say that their little boy compared walks with the great Charlie Chaplin.

We had not entirely finished with Paramount Pictures and we returned the next day, as much to take a look round as anything else. We were given a guided tour of the place and it was quite an eye-opener – especially when we were taken to a set from *Road to Bali* which was in the process of being shot. Bing Crosby was on the set, or rather, off the set – he was sitting in a studio chair fast asleep. Bob Hope was holding court a few feet away, surrounded by script writers. The guide introduced us. He paused in mid-sentence, said, "Hi!", then continued his conversation with his entourage.

About ten years later, I met the terrible twosome, Crosby and Hope, at Shepperton. We were all filming there on different projects. I reminded them of our first meeting during my visit to Hollywood. They admitted that they could remember nothing of our previous meeting but suggested that we could become better acquainted over a drink. We had quite a lot of laughs together and my opinion of them changed. I had thought that they were, per-haps, a little stand-offish – but I was wrong! They were a pair of real jokers and had showbusiness written all the way through them.

It was time for us to return to Britain. I was not sorry, and I did have the feeling that my skirmishes in the States were not over. I had seen the West and had a little success, but it was not yet won. I thought about these things as we flew home. Billy had stocked up with his 'medicine' and I wondered if it would be possible to get Drambuie on prescription.

My second trip to America was over. I was impressed with what I had seen. There was always an air of perpetual optimism and unashamed extravagance about the place. Remember that I had spent many a night sleeping rough on the pavements of London. Such a thing as a luxury suite at the Beverley Wiltshire Hotel did not enter my wildest dreams in those days. I liked American people. They were confident and enthusiastic. They had their moaners and their liars just the same as we do, but generally they were quite friendly and always did their best to make you feel at home.

As I contemplated these things I just knew that I would be going back for more. As it happened, it took quite a few years, and a great deal happened to me in Britain, before the States beckoned again. When the opportunity arose once more, I was well prepared to take full advantage of it.

In early 1965, I was appearing in *The Roar of the Greasepaint – The Smell of the Crowd*. An American director by the name of Cy Feuer came to my dressing-room and asked if I might be interested in a project he was planning for the summer of 1966. His idea was to take *Hobson's Choice* and turn it into a stage musical called *Walking Happy*. It sounded a bit barmy to me, but when he said that he was going to present it on Broadway, I was quite prepared to share his strait-jacket.

After he had gone I didn't think any more about it. With all due respect to him and others, when you are in showbusiness you are regularly targeted by people who offer all sorts of strange projects. Few of them actually materialise for a variety of reasons. I never think badly of people whose ideas don't manage to get off the ground. It has happened to me many times. It is better to have an idea that doesn't happen than to have no idea at all.

This idea, though, was one that did happen. Cy Feuer worked hard back in the States and very soon a contract was on its way. That is why, in the summer of 1966, I was back in the USA to star as Will Mossop in this ambitious production. It might seem to be a tremendous gamble to take Harold Brighouse's classic play set in Salford and present it as an all-singing, all-dancing Broadway Musical – but I suppose it's no different than taking a collection of poems about cats and doing the same thing. In both cases it worked!

I'm not going to be all snooty and tell you that everything was 'simply wonderful Luvvie-dahling!' It wasn't! In fact it was extremely hard work and very difficult at the start. The Americans have a rather different approach to their rehearsals and preparation, and in the initial weeks before the show opened I discovered that they had built up a resentment for me that gradually turned to outright insult. I took it in my stride though!

Once the show finally opened, those same cast members who had been so openly rude were queuing to apologise. We had a big success on our hands and the planned summer season of 1966 at the Lunt-Fontanne Theatre went right on until April 1967 – followed by an extensive tour the length and breadth of the United States. The success of the show was not just at the box-office either. It won a whole range of awards, including two for myself. There were a number of nominations for Tony Awards. I was nominated for Best Actor in a Musical. I didn't expect to win and so was not too disappointed when the great Robert Preston's name came out of the envelope.

The show finally came to an end at the Dorothy Parker Pavilion in Los Angeles. We were there for a month and I was visited by an amazing number of major international stars who just dropped in to say 'hello' after seeing the show. Among these great names were Elizabeth Taylor and Richard Burton, Jerry Lewis, Edward G.Robinson, Mary Tyler Moore and John Wayne.

It was a film buff's dream. Jerry Lewis talked about us doing a film together, Richard Burton congratulated me on my singing, and John Wayne gave me a slap on the back that nearly sent me hurtling across the room.

I also met up again with Joan Crawford. It was at a charity lunch and, if you remember, I had met her before when I was a kid in one of my first jobs. She had given me a kiss then. When I sat next to her at the charity 'do', I told her about it. She was amused and gave me another kiss. Since she put her hand on my knee at the same time, I took it that I was no longer considered in the same light as on our previous encounter. She had a bit of a reputation as a man-eater and I didn't want to be the prey! I treated her as a lady and she treated me as a gentleman – and that's the way it remained.

Oh yes, there was another little experience that was fun. You have probably heard of Graumann's Chinese Theatre – it is famous for having the hand and footprints of the stars in the cement outside. Well, I was asked to go along and make my mark in the cement. They wanted a right hand and a right foot and I was quite happy to oblige. It was quite a thrill to see my prints alongside those of real stars like Judy Garland, Fred Astaire, Douglas Fairbanks, Charlie Chaplin and many, many others.

The only problem with putting your prints into concrete is that you can get set in your ways!

So, was the West well and truly won? Certainly *Walking Happy* was a winner and, once again, I had met up with my old pal Ed Sullivan, who welcomed me to his television show as if we were brothers. He never failed to remind me of my cheek in going to his apartment but, like most Americans, he admired the incident and always said so.

Before *Walking Happy* went on tour I had an unusual visitor to my dressing-room. You get all kinds of visitors when you are at a theatre, but this one was a bit different. I felt that I ought to know him but I was sure that I didn't. He was a well-dressed middle-aged man, very polite and pleasant. He spoke like a fan rather than someone in the business. That's not meant as an insult by the way – it's just that people in the business have a different approach.

Suddenly, as we chatted about the weather, he hit me with a bombshell.

"I'd like you to do a show for me!"

'Oh no, not another one', I thought. I didn't want to be rude but I was whacked out and I didn't need another pipe-dream at that time of night. I remained polite though, and I did my best to sound interested.

"Really! That's nice. What's the show about?"

Thinking back, I must have sounded as if I were trying to humour him – which I suppose I was really!

"It's called *Androcles and the Lion*, he said.

I knew the story very well of course – who doesn't? It is a George Bernard Shaw classic that only top actors usually qualify for. By now, I was convinced that this was no pipe-dream… it was a complete delusion!

"Oh yes, and what would my role be?"

"Androcles of course!" He seemed amazed that I needed to ask.

I just managed to stop myself from laughing out loud, but I was beginning to run out of patience.

"Have you cast it yet?" I steeled myself for the answer.

"Well, I've got Noel Coward to play the Emperor Caesar…!"

This time I did laugh. I told you that we get all sorts visit us. I had tried very hard to be accommodating, but now I had had enough.

"You must excuse me," I said. "I'm very tired and I really must…"

"I'm sorry," he interrupted. "I didn't introduce myself properly Mr Wisdom. Whatever must you be thinking? My name is Richard Rodgers!"

Richard Rodgers! Richard Rodgers – as in *The Sound of Music*, *The King and I*, *South Pacific* and a whole range of other legendary musicals. Now it was my turn to apologise, genuinely sorry that I had failed to recognise him. He waved aside my explanations and, like the gentleman that he was, he out-apologised me. Then he set about explaining that it was to be a special production for NBC television.

Fans of *It'll be Alright On The Night* will appreciate one little memory of that show. We were all in awe of Noel Coward, of course. He was referred to as 'The Master', and willingly accepted such a label. Why should he argue with everyone else's opinion? I had quite a lot of dialogue with him and there were a few funny moments, such as the time I grabbed his toga to stop him walking off his mark, because he had the habit of moving while he was talking.

But the classic for me was the moment he stood in full regalia and, with all the dignity one would expect of the Roman Empire's top man, he addressed the Roman underlings – which for this scene amounted to several hundred extras. He cast his regal eye over his people, raised his arms aloft and began his speech. "Lo and behold," he declared. Then he paused for a moment. "Lo and behold!" Another lengthy pause and then came the momentous announcement. "The Master has forgotten his ******* lines!" The place erupted as several hundred people collapsed in helpless fits of laughter.

Despite those moments, *Androcles and the Lion* was well received. The young lady who played my wife, Megaera, has recently become an even bigger favourite on British television with her portrayal of Hyacinth Bucket in *Keeping up Appearances*. Yes, Androcles' wife was played by Patricia Routledge.

I was still meeting all the stars while I was in the States. Kirk Douglas, Johnny Mathis, Johnny Weismuller, Count Basie, Woody Hermann, Ella Fitzgerald, Dean Martin to name but a few. I'm a real name dropper aren't I? Not really though – we were all on chat shows together. You might think that I became a bit blasé about meeting all these famous people – but I never did! I was still like a little kid. Every time I met a star for the first time, a little voice deep inside me said, "Cor! That's Elizabeth Taylor!", – or Noel Coward or whoever. I never got used to it and I don't think I ever will. I still meet those famous people and it still gives me a big thrill every time.

With *Walking Happy* and *Androcles and the Lion* to my credit, I could have thought that that was the end of my American career – but it wasn't. United Artists signed me to make *The Night They Raided Minsky's*, with Jason Robards, Elliott Gould, Bert Lahr, Forrest Tucker, Denholm Elliott, Harry Andrews, Joseph Wiseman and Britt Ekland.

It was fun to make, even though I had to struggle through one afternoon's filming after Jason Robards had insisted on buying me a large whiskey during the lunchtime break. He not only bought it, but he watched me drink it. I have to tell you that I have never been much of a drinker. I have always preferred a drink of lemonade to a pint of bitter. I will have the occasional drink but I can take it or leave it. When Jason forced me into that whiskey I had never drunk anything stronger than a Pepsi for more than a year. My head was swimming, while Jason was word-perfect. He was well used to breakfast, lunch and supper from a bottle. I wasn't!

The only bit of sadness during the making of the film was the death of Bert Lahr. I had shared scenes with him and had some pleasant chats as well. He died before all his scenes were complete and therefore they were cut out of the film. Possibly his name remains unknown to you, but if I mention the cowardly lion in the fantastic *Wizard of Oz*, you will know exactly who I mean.

The film did well and was given great reviews. *Time Magazine* was very kind to me and said I could be compared favourably with Buster Keaton.

A year later I returned to New York to appear in the farce *Not Now*. The critics gave it a good hiding and it died a death on Broadway. I was not too worried – I had already achieved my success in the USA.

That was how the West was Won! But there was a cost – my marriage!

Meanwhile...

I JUMPED ahead a bit in giving you my own West Side Story so, with your permission, I'll return to the events following Billy and I coming back to England after my first appearance on the *Ed Sullivan Show* and my later, wonderful, meeting with Charlie Chaplin. The press were there to meet us at the airport and that's when Billy brought into play the story that I had said an emphatic "No, no, no, to Hollywood." It did my image good because, at that time, the British public were getting a bit fed-up with the American film giants swallowing up all their favourites.

Billy Marsh was on a roll and I was along for the ride. His next bit of good news was that Bernard Delfont wanted to put me in his new revue, *Paris to Piccadilly*, at the Prince of Wales Theatre. He was to build the show around me and give me my first solo billing in London's West End. In the past I had been just a part of various shows which were sold by their title. In this one, the show title was virtually a caption to my name.

You may remember that I told you how well Eddie Leslie and I had got on during our pantomime season. Well, for *Paris to Piccadilly* he was to be my straight man and, as such, he pioneered the character that was to be played later by Jerry Desmonde and Tony Fayne. As I have already said, David Nixon had been my partner in various straight man and stooge routines, but this was something different.

There was a long panto season at Wolverhampton in which I was Buttons again, and then we were into rehearsals for *Paris to Piccadilly*. That was when the fun started. I have never tried to be 'difficult' – but sometimes, if I feel that something should be done in a certain way, I'll stick to my guns until I am proven wrong – then I'll be the first to sincerely apologise. When I'm proved right, I don't make a big deal out of it – I'm just happy that things have worked out as I had hoped. There are times when you have to fight your corner and this proved to be one of them.

Dickie Hurran, an absolutely brilliant director, was putting the show together. A marvellous man, nobody would question his word – except me of course! I had a thirty-minute spot and was going through my routine at one of the last rehearsals when Dickie suddenly called a halt.

"What are you doing Norman?" He asked. I had just picked up my clarinet.

"I'm playing the clarinet! It's in the act!"

"No you're not!" He replied. "There are twenty-two musicians in the orchestra. We don't need another one. You stick to your comedy Norman!"

The same thing happened when I picked up the sax – and then again when I was going to sing.

"But," I protested. "That's how I finish the act!"

"We don't need the singing! We've got professionals on the show!" Dickie shouted from the stalls.

I suppose that this was the point where I became 'difficult'.

"Dickie, I'm going for a tea break. When I come back I'm doing my full act – the singing, the clarinet, the sax, everything! Now, if you don't want it like that, then I've signed the wrong contract and I'll leave!"

As you will have gathered, I was a bit wound up by this time. I stormed off. Eddie Leslie joined me to calm me down a bit. He was a good listener while I had a real moan over our tea in a local cafe.

"I agree with you Norman! Stick to your guns mate," said Eddie.

When we got back to the theatre, Bernard Delfont was sitting in the stalls with Dickie Hurran.

"Norman, Norman! You've got to listen to what the director says." He spoke soothingly, trying to pacify me.

"I know!" I replied. "I have the greatest respect and admiration for Dickie – but I know my own act and, on this occasion, I believe that I'm right!"

The tension did not ease. In fact, it even started to get to Mr Delfont who tried to throw me an order.

"Just do what the director says!"

I stood my ground and shook my head.

"I'm sorry, but I can't change! You've got the wrong bloke. You'll have to leave me out of the show!"

We seemed to be in a stalemate situation so someone sent for Val Parnell. He arrived and tried the softly, softly approach – explaining that they knew what was best for the show. But I still wouldn't have it. Val Parnell, Bernard Delfont and Dickie Hurran had a chat between themselves and, finally, Val Parnell tried again.

"Look Norman," he pleaded. "The show opens tomorrow. Here's a compromise plan. Do the show our way on the first night, then do it your way on the second. Whichever night goes the best, that's the way we'll keep it for the rest of the run. Now, is that fair enough?"

"No!" I said. "I've got a better idea!"

The peace shattered again as Parnell hit the roof – but I still wouldn't give in.

"I'll tell you what would be fair! On the opening night, let me do it my way. If it doesn't work then we'll do it your way for the rest of the season."

I won the argument and the opening night was soon upon us. I hope this doesn't sound big-headed but I got a standing ovation and three curtain-calls. Dickie Hurran was the first to greet me.

He gave me a big hug and a kiss and we were friends again. No explanations or recriminations were necessary.

Stage show offers came thick and fast. The show at the Prince of Wales ran and ran. Eddie Leslie and I were contracted to appear in *Jack and the Beanstalk* at the Coventry Hippodrome during the Christmas and New Year period, so we left *Paris to Piccadilly*, returning when the panto season finished. While we were away, our places were taken by Archie Robbins and Leslie Randall.

I am always reminded of that Coventry panto whenever I see *The Sound of Music, Mary Poppins, Victor Victoria* and several other similar musical films. Can you spot the connection? Yes!... Julie Andrews! The very talented and lovely Julie Andrews – what a girl! She really was born in a suitcase, because her parents were touring entertainers before she arrived. Julie joined them on stage from almost the moment that she could first walk – and she developed into one of England's greatest entertainers.

I first met her at Coventry in *Jack and the Beanstalk* in that 1952-53 season. She was playing Princess Bettina. She was just eighteen then... oops! Now I've given her age away! She had a wicked sense of fun and used to find lots of different ways of winding me up. Sometimes she would mess up my dressing-room, other times she would jump on my back when I was least expecting it, or she would start to tell me a story that was complete nonsense, just to see how far she could get before I twigged that she was having me on.

We used to sing and dance together in a couple of routines and she was wonderful. I used to have to catch her in my arms during one routine and I began to notice that she was getting heavier – or seemed to be. One day she leaped into my arms and I sank to my knees on the floor.

"You'd better keep off the cakes," I told her. "That is unless of course..."

She just laughed, and then told me how she had a bet on, with one of the other girls, that she would get me on my knees.

113

That was Julie Andrews all over – lots of fun, a great performer and a lovely lady. She still is!

In between the stage-shows and panto, I was also getting more television and radio work. I've already told you about some of the early television shows but there were many more in those early days. In December 1950, for instance, I was the subject of a programme called *Critic's Choice*. It was a 'frightfully posh' effort, which showed me at work and then discussed what I was all about – or rather, what other people thought I was all about. Nice programme!

In March 1951, there was *All The Fun Of The Fair*, with Arthur Askey, Elizabeth Welch, Jerry Desmonde, Renee Houston and Donald Stewart and lots of others. It was really amazing what you could get into an hour-long programme in those days.

In April and May 1951 there was a series called *Vic's Grill* – a half-hour show presented by Vic Wise. Eddie Leslie was in it, John Hanson, Beryl Reid, Ernest Maxin, Rae Johnson, Hamish Menzies and Eric Robinson and his Orchestra. How about that for a memory? Then there were two television shows from the ice extravaganza at the Empress Hall, and two more TV shows in December of that same year. *The Top Hat Rendezvous* was another variety show hosted by Derrick De Marney. Arthur English was on it, Muriel Young, Freddie Sales, Les Richards, Audrey Wayne, the Twelve Toppers and Eric Robinson and the Orchestra.

The final TV show of the year for me was on Christmas Day in the evening. It was appropriately called *Christmas Party*. Leslie Mitchell and Jerry Desmonde hosted the show, and Eric Robinson and the Orchestra were also there of course. The artistes included Terry Thomas, Jimmy Jewel and Ben Warris, David Nixon, Ethel Revnell, Rawicz and Landauer, Petula Clark, Anne Ziegler and Webster Booth and the Twelve Toppers.

In those days, Christmas Day television was live, not like today when so much is recorded months ahead, then wrapped around the Queen's speech and a couple of blockbuster movies.

When you were working on Christmas Day you were determined to enjoy it and I honestly believe that those early TV shows did much to enhance a family's day. I can't help feeling that, nowadays, the TV has reached the stage where it causes arguments as to what to watch, or just provides a background for people to snore away their indigestion. But then, what do I know?... I'm just a berk!

The television shows continued and still continue. Radio, too, gave me a great opportunity to try out fresh ideas. If you trip over on radio, very few people see it. Therefore there had to be much more patter, using the voice to paint the picture. There were all kinds of radio shows too – *Blackpool Pirates* was a children's show with Charlie Chester, Frankie Howerd, Jimmy Jewel and Ben Warris and a whole lot of other names. That was in August 1949 and it was repeated a fortnight later. Then there was a contrast in *Henry Hall's Guest Night, Band Parade, Fine Goings On* and many other radio productions during the late 1940s and early '50s. I have been a radio regular ever since.

Back in my early radio days, the *Radio Times* decided to give me another mention: 'Norman Wisdom, a delightful clown who can talk gibberish with agonised animation!'

I suppose that was some sort of compliment.

I'm going to talk about the films in a little while but for now there are still a few more tales about the live shows. At the end of the *Paris to Piccadilly* show, I was told to get my skates on again and return to the Empress Hall for *Sinbad the Sailor*, in which I was cast, I can't imagine why, as – Norman!

Having so much space and seating for ten thousand people, Claude Langdon was able to promote a real extravaganza and *Sinbad* was the sort of show that gave a pretty free hand to the director and choreographer. Andra McLaughlin was in the title role, a lovely girl – Andra that is – and a lovely skater. Eve Bradfield wrote and produced the show – and choreographed it as well – a real busy lady, especially when you consider that there were ninety-six entertainers involved – plus the orchestra.

One of my favourite moments was driving on to the ice in a model T-Ford. It looked for all the world as if I was not looking where I was going and, strictly speaking, I didn't! But there was a trick to it. I was actually watching the ceiling because there were marks there which told me where to drive and where to stop. It looked heart-stopping from the audience's point of view – especially those in the front row, who thought that I was going to drive straight into them.

I injured myself in this show. I was well-used to getting bruises, but it was very rare for me to get really hurt. It was a trampoline routine that caused the damage. I mistimed a somersault and ended up landing head-first on the ice. As a result of the mishap I began to lose the use of my left arm and I began to get a bit concerned. It turned out to be a trapped nerve and a chipped bone. I had to have a minor operation to put it right.

I took great pride in never missing a show and I didn't want to start now, so I arranged to have the operation on a Sunday when we didn't have a performance. I did have to take it a little easier for a few days, but at least I kept up my record of never missing a show.

One of the things about my career that I have really enjoyed is the diversity. The theatre shows, television, radio, films and the ice-shows all presented quite different challenges – and I've always loved a challenge. I soon got my 'ice-legs' back for *Sinbad* and had a great season.

Next came *Sketches and Variety* at the Birmingham Hippodrome, with Jerry Desmonde and Joan Reagan. This was followed by the wonderful London Palladium which really deserves a chapter all to itself.

My first appearance at the London Palladium was in 1954, with Jerry Desmonde, Walter Wahl, The Three Monarchs, Gillian Moran and Teddy Hale. Dickie Hurran produced it and, for me, it was sheer magic to be appearing on the world's most wonderful stage. To be appearing on that stage where so many of the great legends of showbusiness had set foot before me – and since, of course – was something which I can hardly put into words. The Palladium is special – a gorgeous, lovely theatre, the palace of stars.

It's an interesting venue because it used to be a circus building, especially created to present that unique form of entertainment at its best. I think that it was in 1910 that the Palladium finally became the theatre that we all know and love today. It is not only held in great esteem and affection in this country, the Palladium has become famous throughout the world. When you read through the list of great stars who have appeared there, that esteem comes as no surprise. Frank Sinatra, Bob Hope, Bing Crosby, Danny Kaye, Judy Garland, Michael Jackson – they have all appeared at the Palladium.

Comedians love to play at the Palladium because of the way the laughter rolls around the auditorium and comes back to you, encouraging you on to even greater effort. At many theatres, the sound goes out and stays out, but the very shape of the Palladium means that it collects the sound and builds it up.

One of the biggest laughs I ever had in showbusiness was at the Palladium. The great curtain was operated by water pressure and, during one sketch that I was doing with Jerry Desmonde, the curtain began to close. What had happened was that a water main had burst outside in the street and had caused low water pressure inside the building. When we saw the curtains slowly closing, Jerry and I began to talk faster. We thought that if we got a move on we might just complete the sketch before the curtain finally closed. So we were gabbling away like a speeded up record, the band were in hysterics, the audience were roaring as they realised what was happening and, to cap it all, Jerry and I got a fit of the giggles as we rattled off our lines. When the curtain finally closed completely we were on the floor, helplessly laughing our heads off. I still have a good laugh when I think about it now.

When I was at the Palladium I used to take my props up to the bar when everyone else had gone home. Everyone used to think that I was raving mad, but I wanted to be as near perfect as I could. Robert Nesbitt was director at the time and he was particularly interested in lighting – he liked to set it himself for the show. In fact, he was nicknamed 'The Prince Of Darkness'. He always worked late and took pride in the fact that he worked later than everyone else. One night, when I was into full swing with my practice, at about 2.30am, Robert popped into the bar to see me and said, "Good night Norman!... You win!"

I'd worked later than Robert Nesbitt – it was unheard of!

That season at the Palladium was not my very first appearance there. I had already appeared there for a Royal Variety Show in 1952. But it was the first time that I had worked a full season there – and as top of the bill!

I was back there again in 1955 in a show called *Painting The Town*. We had already toured it in Amsterdam, Brighton, Birmingham and Liverpool and so, by the time we arrived at the Palladium, we were in full swing. Jerry Desmonde, Ruby Murray, Pauline Chamberlain, Nanci Crompton, June Ellis and the George Mitchell Singers were in the programme, which was another produced by Dickie Hurran.

And so it went on! Television, radio, the stage. I even made a guest appearance in a special charity performance of Bertram Mills Circus at Olympia in 1957. It was a busy time all right.

There was another departure at the end of 1957 when I was asked to appear in *Where's Charley?* – which was a musical version of *Charley's Aunt*, the well-known classic story. When I was cast as Charley Wykeham, the critics rubbed their hands with glee. They couldn't wait to see me flop. I don't think it was because of any personal animosity toward me, but they didn't like the idea of an uncouth entertainer – who gets his living by falling over – getting a legitimate part. Snooty lot!

It was a new experience for me and I was helped by having Jerry Desmonde in the cast as Sir Francis Chesney and the experienced Pip Hinton as Amy. The critics were disappointed because the production worked well and it actually ran for eighteen months. It was quite different from my previous stage experience and I was now able to add musical farce to my theatrical CV.

The Roar Of The Greasepaint – The Smell Of The Crowd was conceived by Anthony Newley and Leslie Bricusse. Tony Newley also directed and I played a character called 'Cocky'. I have to say that I was disappointed – very disappointed – with the way it turned out. For once I took complete direction, in that I didn't put any of my own ideas into the show. Tony Newley knew what he wanted and that was that! I feel that I must be allowed to put a few ideas in, or at least talk them over with the director before trying them out. It taught me a lesson.

I have never had a year without theatre shows, television and radio – but I won't go into the details of every single show if you don't mind. It would turn this book into a directory.

There is one other of the old shows that many people ask me about. The much-loved and sadly-missed *Sunday Night At The London Palladium*. I appeared on the show more than once but, it seems, most people remember the night of 3 December 1961. There was an Equity dispute at the time and it looked as if the show might well have to be cancelled. I had already signed a contract to appear on that night so I didn't imagine that Equity would make too much fuss as it would be wrong to break a contract. I talked to Billy Marsh.

"Billy, if Bruce is willing to have a go, I'll do the whole hour with him – just him and me!"

Bruce, of course, was Bruce Forsyth, then, the resident compère of *Sunday Night At The London Palladium*. Billy phoned Val Parnell who thought that it was a crazy idea but was prepared to risk it if I was.

I phoned Bruce and asked him how he felt about it, explaining that we would have to work for a week solid to rehearse it. Bruce said that he was prepared for that, which I knew he would because he is a real professional and has never shirked hard work. So we took the bull by the horns and worked for hours, day after day, for the entire week leading up to the show.

One routine in particular was to be done as a silent, slapstick number. Bruce wasn't sure at first but, after we had run through it a few times, he warmed to it and launched himself into totally mastering it. I have said thanks to Bruce before, both privately and publicly. I have taken another look at that video recently and it still stands up as a classic, of which I am very proud. But it was you that made it Bruce and I'm still grateful for all those long hours, the hard work and the fun we had in putting it together. If that same situation should ever arise again Bruce – let's make sure that you and I are – OUT OF THE COUNTRY!

The show began with its theme-tune overture. Those of you who remember the show will need no prompting as to how it went. You will probably also remember Bruce's famous catch-phrase, "I'm in charge!". Well, we started the show with me running through the audience wearing a large badge with Bruce's catch-phrase written on it in huge letters. Bruce chased me until we reached the stage. Then I had to tell a joke without laughing if I wanted to stay. Of course I failed, but I pleaded for another chance.

I was then given a lesson in rhythm, using a particularly painful method. It was a great prop – and still is. I am still using it in my shows today. I acquired it in 1954 when Bernard Delfont saw it in use in America and bought the rights to the gag, just because he thought it would be a good gag for me. It still gets lots of laughs and I still get lots of bruises. It got a lot of laughs on that special *Sunday Night at the London Palladium*.

The main sketch, however, was an eleven-minute wall-papering routine in which Bruce was the foreman and I was his idiot assistant. This is the one that worried Bruce. It was done in total silence except for the background music and the roars of laughter from the audience. Yes, they loved it and, judging by the letters we received, so did the millions of viewers.

At the end of that one-hour show we took our place on the famous revolving stage – and we received a standing ovation. It was one of the most enjoyable things that I have ever done – a tremendous challenge that, quite easily, could have gone terribly wrong.

A few pages back I mentioned having done a Christmas Day television show called *Christmas Party*. I was on that show in 1951, 1952 and 1953 – but it was the first one that was to have such a profound affect on my life. It was watched by a man named Earl St John. As he sat at home on Christmas night, watching the box with his family, he began to get a few ideas whizzing through his head. It was really good news for me because Earl St John was the senior executive producer of the Rank Organisation!

The Pictures

WHEN Billy Marsh came into my dressing-room with a face as long as a cucumber, during the *Roar of the Greasepaint* show, I suspected that there was bad news on the way. If it was likely to be good news then Billy would have been bubbling over and eager to tell me. This time, however, he was awkward and seemed to be putting off the inevitable. As I told you earlier, there had been problems with the show – and I just knew inside that Billy had come to tell me that it was coming to a premature close.

Looking down at his shoes he murmured, "I've got some very bad news Norman and I'm not sure that I know how to tell you!"

"Just come straight out with it!" I urged, wondering what could be so bad.

His face lifted and he looked me straight in the eye. Then he smiled. The smile turned into a big grin and then he began to laugh.

"The Rank Organisation want to sign you to a seven-year film contract!"

I was stunned! Of course I had heard a whisper or two, but in this business you don't take whispers too seriously. When Billy hit me with this development you could have knocked me down with the proverbial feather.

Billy's brilliant management skills, of course, had once again played a major part in this new adventure. Earl St John had indeed watched *Christmas Party* on television. He had seen his family's reaction to Norman Wisdom and had decided that I just might have something to offer the big screen. Rank were not in very good shape at that time. It was chiefly because of a political move by the British Government of the day, who had decided to slap a 75 per cent tax on all foreign films coming into the country from August 1947. The idea behind the tax was that, since the Americans were by far the biggest earners from British cinemas, a flow of cash out of the country through that medium might be diverted. The Government also hoped that the Americans would use the loophole of investment in British films – which would, in turn, create extra employment and go to keeping the cash in Britain.

The Americans did not fall for that one though! They simply blocked their films coming to Britain and also put a ban on British films being shown in the USA. The British Government played its next card by encouraging British producers to fill the void left by the lack of American films by creating more of their own for the market. Rank were very happy to do their bit and announced a £9 million investment, with a view to creating forty-seven films. Then the Government renewed talks with the Americans and a deal was struck!

Rank now found itself in the situation of having over-stretched itself financially, only to find that the floodgates had been opened and their films were being drowned in the deluge of American movies that were now being let into the country. It was an extremely awkward position. Rank, as well as being film-makers, also owned a chain of cinemas. They could not refuse to show American films because that would have seriously damaged their cinema business. Neither could they turn back from their investment programme – because too much money had already been spent. It was quite a dilemma!

In the end, the only answer was cut-backs, and John Davis, administrator and accountant, was just the man to do it. All executives took a pay cut, studios at Islington, Denham and Shepherd's Bush were closed down and, gradually, Rank was able to pull back from the brink. In October 1948, Rank had been £13.5 million in the red and losing money every week. By January 1951, the tide had begun to turn and Rank were no longer losing money.

That was the situation into which I was happily walking in 1952, when Billy Marsh so cunningly hinted to the Rank Organisation that their rivals, Associated British Cinemas, were on the verge of offering me a contract! Rank immediately put a deal together which guaranteed me three films in the first two years of a seven-year agreement. The first film would yield me £5,000!

In May 1952, Rank were still in debt to the tune of £9 million, but had twenty-two films in production. It was make or break time for them – and if they went down the pan they could well take me with them as far as my reputation was concerned. Rank had no actual films lined up for me when I signed contracts with them. I didn't even have to do a screen test before they agreed to sign me. It was all an incredible gamble!

Was I excited at the prospect of getting into films?... Not 'arf!

I wasn't the only one. The film press were soon told and they also gave me a nice welcome to their industry.

Eventually, of course, the inevitable screen test did come along. I was summoned to the famous Pinewood Studios and so I decided to look the part. No, I didn't wear dark glasses – but I did swank my way through the big wrought-iron gates in my new two-tone Bentley. I didn't really know what my screen test would entail and so I was delighted, upon my arrival, to find that it was to be a brief scene with Petula Clark. We knew each other well – so that was good news. I knew that we would be able to work well together.

Next came the bad news! The script was not only dreadful – it was straight! I had been contracted for comedy and they gave me a deadpan couple of lines that were totally uninspiring, even though I was playing opposite lovely Pet Clark. Ronald Neame was the director and he was to be in charge of my first film.

If I told you that we hit it off from the start then I would be telling you a giant-sized fib! The truth is that we didn't get on at all! He was an expert in the field of film drama, while I was pretty expert in the field of knockabout comedy – and ne'er the twain shall meet, as they say! It was far from an ideal situation and so my disappointment was tinged with some relief when the first film was cancelled and I was paid off – but only for the first film.

Time went by and nothing seemed to be happening. There were even suggestions that Rank wanted to pay us off and cancel the contract – but we had come too far and we kept to our side of the bargain. We were available to make films – it was up to them to put us to work! In August 1952, *Picturegoer* magazine heightened the embarrassment when they reported that there was nothing much happening even though Rank had signed a contract three months earlier. It was suggested that Rank were going to make a cash settlement and tear up the contract.

I was concerned, of course. Getting paid for doing nothing is all very well – and there have been times when it's been the other way about and I have worked my backside off without getting paid – but the point was, I wanted to do the films. I had never forgotten how much I had enjoyed being with that film crew for those few precious hours on the sea front at Deal, when I was a boy. Even though I hadn't recognised it then, something had stirred deep inside myself. There was a pilot-light somewhere inside me – a deep yearning to be involved in that sort of work. The contract with the Rank Organisation had been the potential fulfilment of that yearning. Someone had lit the gas from that pilot-light and now I wanted something to cook and produce from this burning desire for the silver screen.

Rank assured me that they were not going to pull out of their contract with me. I took them at their word even though it was probably a bit like the 'vote of confidence' that football managers get just before they're sacked. We were at stalemate though – the ideas for a film in which Rank were prepared to invest were a bit thin on the ground. Earl St John stuck by his original thought, however, and turned to a scriptwriter named Jill Craigie. If I tell you that she was also known as Mrs Michael Foot, wife of the man who later became leader of the Labour Party, you will probably be surprised. Jill Craigie was a very talented lady and she certainly delivered the goods!

Jill came up with a story about a department store – or should that be departmental store (one week there and you depart – mental!). The story-line had many opportunities for my sort of humour and, as I began to read the first draft, I started to smile, then to chuckle and, before long, I was having a really good laugh. It was a great idea and I could visualise my character getting into all sorts of scrapes.

John Paddy Carstairs, a great writer and director, was given the job of bringing the idea to life. He added Ted Willis and Maurice Cowan to the team, and between them they beefed up the film which became known as *Trouble In Store*. It was a simple idea – but then, most of the best notions work because of their simplicity. I was happy because I have always been a very simple person!

My character, Norman, (I never did have a surname in that film), is the very down-to-earth assistant in the store's stockroom. He is not thick but he is a little – no, a lot – naive. His great ambition is to become a window-dresser for this mighty emporium called Burridges. Not only would that be a big step up the ladder for Norman, but it would also, he thinks, get him noticed by the young lady who has stolen his heart – Sally, who was played by Lana Morris.

Jerry Desmonde played the fire-breathing new head of the store and Norman was continually running into trouble with him. I was sacked and reinstated so many times that, if it was in real life, they would have given me my own revolving doors! It provided countless opportunities for my visual, slapstick humour – right from the opening scene, which has become so famous since it has been used so often as a clip whenever I am being interviewed on chat shows.

The opening scene shows the store chief sitting in his

chauffeur-driven convertible limo with me alongside him – or at least that is how it appears. The car is at traffic-lights and, when they change, the vehicle moves off, making it obvious that I was alongside the car on my bike. It got a great laugh right at the start of the film and set the mood and the tone for the next eighty-five minutes.

One of my favourite scenes is where I am called to the boss's office. I don't recognise him and he doesn't really recognise me from our earlier exchange at the traffic lights. I assume that he is also waiting to see the boss and decide that we should have a bit of fun while we are waiting. I help myself to his cigars and urge him to do the same. I lounge back in his chair and put my feet on his desk, rearrange his papers, impersonate him and generally fool around until the chief finally explodes by yelling for his secretary (Moira Lister) and sacking me there and then.

The reason that I had been called to the office in the first place was because the mighty new chief had wanted to show his human side to the staff by meeting the lowliest of all the employees. Within minutes the exasperated boss had given way to his real self and given lowly Norman the boot! Not for long though!

The film was unique in that it had two of my regular straight men taking part. Jerry Desmonde was the boss, as I've already said, but Eddie Leslie was also in the film as a would-be robber. Derek Bond was my rival for the attentions of Sally and there was a cast of other box-office faithfuls like Megs Jenkins, Joan Sims and Michael Ward. And, of course, there was another star, who had carefully and cleverly been put into the plot to guarantee getting noticed by the cinema-going public – Margaret Rutherford!

By the time *Trouble In Store* was made, Margaret was sixty-one years old and already had twenty years of film experience. She was a great help to me, almost mothering me at times, as I learned the trade. She was a brilliant actress with wonderful abilities in comedy. In this film she played the part of an eccentric titled lady who enjoyed shoplifting. She was sheer magic, both to watch and to work with, and I learned so much from her in those early days.

Trouble In Store was shot at Pinewood in the summer of 1953. I hit it off with Paddy Carstairs from the start. We didn't agree on everything – far from it – but he had a great sense of humour and he showed due respect to everyone, from the star to the tea-lady. He also helped me a lot in those nervous early days. I had been filmed once before, some years earlier, when I did my shadow-boxing routine at Collins Music Hall for a film called, *A Date With A Dream*. That was only an incidental part in which I appeared for all of thirteen seconds. It was nothing like this. My butterflies had always wanted to be in the movies and they were determined not to miss out on this one!

Paddy Carstairs knew that I was very nervous and, after a few days, he took me to one side and said, "Norman, we know you're a hard worker, and we're all chums, but I want to tell you something. I've spent the last three days filming nothing!"

Surprised?... You bet I was! We had been filming all right – and there was film in the cameras – but Paddy had been using it just for test purposes and to help me to get used to being in front of the cameras on a film set – which is different again from television work. Paddy had recognised my inexperience and my nervousness and had used the time to help me settle in. It was a kind of rehearsal time in which to break in Norman the Novice. It worked brilliantly because I became much more relaxed when we started to go through the scenes for real.

It was hard work, especially since I was still appearing each evening at the Prince of Wales for twice-nightly performances of *Paris to Piccadilly*. When we finished the day's filming, I would jump into a chauffeur-driven car at about 5pm and drive to the theatre, where I had to be ready for the first performance at 6.15pm. It was touch and go sometimes but I never missed a performance. There was one occasion when we were stuck in a traffic jam at Marble Arch and it looked as if we were not going to make it in time. I dived out of the car and sprinted through the crowded streets, arriving at the theatre just as the orchestra began playing my music. I went straight on to the stage looking rather dishevelled and out of breath and everyone thought it was all a part of the act. It was a bit of a laugh when I looked back at it because, as I ran through the streets, people were cheering me on and shouting encouragement – almost as if I were going for gold in the Olympic Games!

Back on the set, Paddy and I were having our moments. There is a famous sequence in the store window in which I try to outdo the window-dresser, who was played with just the right amount of bitchy petulance by Michael Ward. Paddy had a habit of throwing his hat on the floor and kicking it when he got angry – and he certainly put the boot into that poor old titfer when I disagreed with him over that scene. He wanted it done in a certain way but I argued that Norman would do it in a different way. After much hat-throwing and kicking, I suggested that we film it both ways and then select whichever way seemed to come over best. Paddy agreed, and in the end I was forced to admit that the best way to play the scene was... mine! Fortunately, Paddy agreed too!

He got his own back later though. It was when we had to film a scene in which I got a soaking in a duck-pond. Every time we filmed it, it wasn't quite right. Paddy had me in and out of that duck-pond six times. Each time I had to change into dry clothes and then go and get soaked again. The whole crew were in hysterics before I twigged what was happening. The very first take had been perfect and was 'in the can', but Paddy kept pretending that it wasn't quite as he wanted it just to wind me up. Revenge was ultimately mine when I rushed at him, picked him up, and carried him to the pond for a ducking of his own.

I felt that the film needed a song. I suppose it was mostly because I liked to include a song in my act but, apart from that, something kept telling me to push for a singing chance in *Trouble*

In Store. When I spoke to Paddy about it I discovered that he had already had the same idea himself.

"Yes Norman, I think that there is a scene which lends itself to a song. The store has a record-booth and Norman could sing to Sally there – perhaps telling of his affection for her and appealing for hers. All we need now is the right song!"

"I've got one!" I said. I quite enjoy song-writing and had already written and performed a couple of numbers in my stage show – *Beware* and *Cinderella Man*.

Paddy rejected my song before I'd even told him what it was about.

"What!" He cried. "Let me see, Norman. You're the star of the film. You do your own stunts. You rewrite the script, and now you want to do the music as well? Don't be daft! You can't do everything!"

So that was me, well and truly put in my place!... Or was it? I took my song to the studios the next day and cornered a young pianist that I had spoken to before.

"Hey Mike! How would you like to do both of us a favour?"

I must have had that look in my eye because I could see him trying vainly to look for the exit. At last he realised that there could be no escape and he gritted his teeth and replied, as cheerfully as possible, "Sure Norman! What have you got in mind?"

"Have a look at this song! Then run through it a few times so that you can play it if you're asked. Scribble your name on it and then take it to Paddy Carstairs. Tell him that you heard that he was looking for a song for Norman Wisdom and ask him if this one might be of any use. You'll have to see what happens then and play it by ear!"

Later that day a triumphant Paddy Carstairs approached me waving a familiar piece of paper in the air.

"I've got a song for you Norman! I think it could be just the one we're looking for to use in that scene I was talking about. Let's go to the music room and give it a try."

"What's it called?" I asked, very innocently of course.

"Never mind about that!" Paddy was impatient. "Let's hear it first!"

The pianist ran through it for us.

"What do you think?" Paddy was unable to control his excitement at what he believed could be a winner.

"Well, er... umm... I'm not really sure!" I replied, adding frustration to his obvious excitement.

"Well I do!... You're singing it and that's final!" Paddy was insistent. "We're having no arguments on this one!"

"Oh, all right then," I reluctantly agreed.

It was only after the song had been recorded and that we were at the point of no return that I made a full confession to Paddy. I could not possibly repeat what he said!

If you haven't already guessed, the song went something like this –

"Don't laugh at me, 'cos I'm a fool..."

Yes, it was the song that has stayed with me ever since. It was a big hit in the film and it reached the top spot in the record charts and stayed in the Top Ten songs for nine months. I love that song and I can honestly say that I get a lump in my throat every time I sing it – or even when I hear the music. You would think that, by now, I would have heard it enough times for it not to affect me – but it still does. It has been very, very special to me!

Finally the day arrived when we heard those immortal words from the director – "That's a wrap folks!" The filming of *Trouble In Store* was over. Now came nail-biting time. There was a lot at stake on that little film. My career could have been seriously damaged by what the Americans would have called 'a turkey'. The revival of the Rank Organisation was also at stake, they could not have withstood a flop. The nervous tension of production was as nothing compared to the nail-biting suspense of waiting for the reaction of the critics – and to the much-more-important views of the public.

We all assembled at the Gaumont Cinema in Camden Town on 25 November 1953 for a low-key preview – to see if we had the right product for a major release. The public were admitted and there were a couple of rows reserved for the high-ranking executives of the Rank Organisation. As I stayed in the foyer watching them all go in, three or four nodded and about half of these actually remembered my name. "Good evening, Mr Wisdom!" was about the longest conversation that any of them afforded me.

I took my place just as the lights went down and I held my breath. I could hear the two rows of executives and their wives also taking a deep breath as the film began to roll. There on the big screen were Jerry Desmonde and myself appearing to share the limo. The car moved away and the audience saw me on the bike. There was a roar of laughter and two rows of executives and their wives – and little Norman – were heard to breathe out. I knew from that very first reaction that it was going to work, and that *Trouble In Store* was going to be a success.

Throughout the film the audience howled and, at the end, they did something which is rarely experienced in a cinema – they gave me a standing ovation. First of all they cheered and clapped but, when the lights came up and they spotted me at the back of the auditorium, they all stood up. I could have cried and very nearly did!

I went back out to the foyer to find myself surrounded by well-wishers and autograph-hunters – not to mention all those Rank executives and their wives, all of whom had miraculously remembered my first name and that I had a hand which they could shake. The four-word conversation turned into eulogies, lit up by words such as, 'wonderful', 'marvellous', 'hysterical', 'brilliant'.

Of course, it was all very nice and reassuring, and I hope that I don't sound too much like an old cynic when I say that I was very well aware of what the reaction might have been had the film not been so well received. I became pals with a number of those people from Rank but I never allowed myself to stray from what I perceive as the realities of life. Any football manager will tell you that you are only as good as your last result.

So, the scene was set for the release of *Trouble In Store*. Because it was Christmas it was decided not to have a big West End première but to send it straight out with a mass release. In London it was showing in sixty-seven cinemas and fifty-one of these broke their box-office records. The same thing happened in the provinces and even the national newspaper critics went overboard with their praise. I collected the press-cuttings and was particularly pleased with the *Evening Standard's* words, which said: 'It is impossible to avoid comparison with the early Chaplin, for there is much in common between them. It establishes Norman Wisdom as potentially the greatest living comedian of the screen.'

It reminded me of what Charlie Chaplin himself had said when we met. To me he was still the Sorcerer, while I was merely the Apprentice – but to be mentioned in the same breath as the maestro was quite a thrill.

I also received the British Film Academy Award for the Most Promising Newcomer, and that was also a night to remember. Not only was it a glittering affair at the Odeon, Leicester Square, but it was my first acting award.

I felt a tremendous sense of achievement. When I held that award after receiving it, a whole rush of names went through my mind – Paddy Carstairs, Jerry Desmonde, Billy Marsh, my mum, Margaret Rutherford, Eddie Leslie, Lew Lake – almost everyone who had played a part flashed through my head like one of those flicker-books that you used to see. *Trouble In Store* had opened up another world to me. Now I was ready to take on that world again – whatever was 'In Store'!

Court Jester

PERHAPS the greatest accolade that an entertainer can receive is that of being invited to perform in front of royalty. I am proud to say that I have had that experience on a number of occasions. In these days of anti-everything, I find it distressing to see so much of the British heritage literally being destroyed or being the victim of character assassination. Our Royal Family is an integral part of our British heritage. We are all human and we all have our good and bad points but, if someone in the public eye makes a mistake then they are never allowed to forget it. Perhaps if we all concentrated on each other's good points, instead of the bad, we would all get on so much better – there again, I'm just a gump, perhaps I'm talking nonsense!

Anyway, the Royal Family are people just like the rest of us – in fact they are extremely 'human'. Of course, when you are in their company, there are certain 'do's' and 'don't's', but in general you can relax with them and be yourself just as much as when you're with other people. And one thing that was very important to me – every one of them has a great sense of humour!

To give you an example… Everyone's favourite for quite a few years now has been the Queen Mother. That is no disrespect to any of the other members of the Royal Family, it's just because she has been around the longest and, for the older generation, there are many vivid memories of her during the war years – while, for the younger generation, she is admired for the courage she has shown in keeping up her public appearances and duties despite all those illnesses that come with old age. She is just about the perfect image of everyone's favourite Grandma!

Well, my favourite encounter with her was at a charity show, outdoors at Hatfield House in Hertfordshire. It was a sort of garden party and both Eddie Leslie and I were there to perform a routine. The only problem was the weather. It absolutely chucked it down! It didn't rain continuously, but when it came it rained heavily enough to have floated an aircraft carrier on the lawn! Nobody seemed to care though! Whenever the clouds burst everyone dived for cover in the marquees and, when it cleared, they all ventured back into the sunshine. Of course, it was a top-hat and tails job – and that was only the ladies!

Eddie and I were standing in one of the marquees chatting to a few people when I noticed a big dip in the canvas roof. It was obviously full of water and the way that canvas was straining it seemed to me that there was a real danger of it bursting through. So, being a helpful sort of chap, I borrowed a walking stick and gently pushed it against the bulging canvas. It certainly did the trick and sent gallons of water cascading down the side of the marquee from off the roof. I had saved the day! How was I to know that there was a group of ever-so-smartly-dressed ladies and gentlemen standing in direct line of fire? It wasn't really my fault that they all got soaked from the tops of their finely-coiffeured heads to the soles of their well-heeled shoes, now was it?

The Queen Mother had seen the entire incident and she thought it was hysterical. She came over to me and said, "I saw you do that you little tinker!" She got her laughter under control and moved away again – just in case she got part of the blame!

I have met the Queen quite a few times at charity functions, premières and other special events. I don't exactly get a kiss and a hug from her, but she always makes an acknowledgement and says, "Hello again!". I was once told that when she sees me she finds it hard to keep a straight face because I always bring to her mind the comedy routines and films that she has seen that have made her laugh so much. She also may possibly remember an incident at Windsor Castle, even though it was a good many years ago.

I was invited to Windsor Castle for a private show on 17 December 1954. It was meant to be a kind of staff Christmas party but, as was usual, all the Royal Family were there as well. They all muck in together. On this particular occasion, Sid Philips was there with the band and they played quite a selection for both listening to and for dancing. All the members of the Royal Family let their hair down with the staff, dancing with them and joining in with the games. I remember that the Queen particularly liked her dance music to be up-tempo – rather than just sticking to the waltzes.

Wilfred Pickles was compère on this show and had everyone involved in a singalong. Magician Vic Perry did a spot as a pick-pocket which went very well. Prince Philip seemed to be part-icularly keen on watching Vic's expertise. There was a lovely atmosphere in that beautifully decorated room, which was known as the Waterloo Chamber.

It was soon my turn to meet my 'Waterloo'. I had a twenty-minute spot and it went really well. At the end, I couldn't resist walking down the steps from the stage and bowing directly to the Queen, who was sitting in the centre of the front row. She returned my gesture with a lovely smile and that was it!... Well, not quite it! You see, in my excitement and my desire to pay a personal tribute to Her Majesty, I had quite forgotten that it is just not done to turn your back on her. As a result I had to return to the stage by walking backward up the steps. It was easier said than done!

I kept my eyes firmly upon Her Majesty and began the difficult process of returning to the stage, doing my level best to retrace my steps. It was only when I saw the Queen's royal hands go to her royal face that I realised that I was heading for a right royal disaster! I backed straight into a beautiful flower arrangement in a very expensive-looking vase. It tottered and swayed for what seemed ages while everyone in the room watched with utter horror. It was so quiet that you could have heard a pin drop as everyone held their breath. That frozen silence was shattered into more pieces than the vase itself, which took on the appearance of a bone-china jig-saw puzzle, as it finally crashed to the floor.

Her Majesty was stunned! The rest of the Royal Family, too, were struck dumb. No one in the entire room moved or spoke! I looked at the mess on the plush carpet, looked back at the Queen and gave her, what I hoped was, a reassuring smile, and said, "Don't worry Your Majesty... I'll pay for it!"

That broke the silence and the Queen laughed louder than anyone in the room. I beat a hasty, red-faced exit – I had got away with it!

Did I pay?... No I didn't! I offered of course but I was told that it would not be necessary – a pity really since it would have been quite nice to think that the Queen was using a vase that I had bought for her!

I have met most of the Royal Family at *Royal Variety Shows* or the *Royal Command Performance* as it used to be known.

My first *Royal Variety Show* was in 1952. The atmosphere behind the scenes during these shows is always very tense and, sure enough, my butterflies didn't let me down on that night – 3 November 1952. The Queen and the Duke of Edinburgh were there that night. Queen Elizabeth had not yet been crowned at that stage, but she had become Queen immediately on her father's death the previous February and so was doing her best to fulfil all the required engagements, of which this was one. It was hard work for someone so young and still in mourning for her father – but didn't she do a great job!

Val Parnell and Prince Littler put the show together and had assembled a tremendous programme for that night. It was not only my first *Royal Variety Show* but was also my first appearance at the London Palladium. Scared?... Was I scared?... Me?

I was a wreck! There was one consolation – I wasn't alone! everyone on the bill was shaking so much that passers-by must have thought that there was an imminent earthquake!

The show included American stars Howard Keel and The Deep River Boys but, in those days, the show was mostly crammed with British artistes. Behind the scenes there is sheer pandemonium and not only is it a crammed running order – so are the dressing-rooms crammed too. If you have ever seen the Marx Brothers film *A Night At The Opera*, you will probably remember the scene in which there are a mass of people packed into one tiny ship's cabin. In the end, one person too many attempts to open the door and a mêlée of bodies, arms and legs tumble out on to the floor. That's what the backstage dressing-rooms are like at a *Royal Variety Show*! I think we had about eight sharing our one, tiny room. I didn't mind too much except that I kept banging my head against the chain!

Another good thing about a *Royal Variety Show* is that it brings together entertainers who would never otherwise have the chance of working with each other. No promoter could possibly afford to pay such a vast cross section of the entertainment world, and so the *Royal Variety Show* often gives the chance for you to appear with stars who you might otherwise only meet socially.

If you take the 1952 season as an example. I opened the performance with three great people, an act called Jo, Jac and Joni. The idea was that we were four cleaners sweeping the stage ready for the show. The curtain goes up and we are amazed to see a full house staring at us. The other three scarper and I am left on my own. That, of course, is when I go into my routine. It was a great spot for me because the *Royal Variety Show* is also unique in that the opening and closing acts are the ones with the biggest impact on the public. In most shows, the opening acts are pretty well forgotten by the time the interval is over.

On that great night in 1952 there was a tremendous galaxy of stars. Arthur Askey, Tony Hancock, the Crazy Gang, Jimmy Jewel and Ben Warris, Ted Ray, Max Bygraves, Jimmy Edwards, Terry

Thomas, Vic Oliver, the Beverley Sisters, Jack Jackson, Gigli, Josef Locke, Joy Nichols, Pat Kirkwood, the Three Monarchs, Billy Cotton, Jerry Desmonde, Winifred Atwell, Gracie Fields, Vera Lynn and many others who, I hope, will forgive me for not fitting them all in.

I well remember Howard Keel asking me if I was at all nervous before the show. I was, of course, but I noticed that he appeared to be talking rather strangely. The tension had got to him. His mouth was so dry that his lips were sticking to his gums. He was scared stiff and didn't know what to do.

"Here, put some of this on your gums," I said, giving him my tin of Vaseline. It was a little trick that I had learned some time before, and it had never let me down. He took my advice, went on and sang his heart out to rapturous applause. When he came off stage he gave me a big hug and a kiss.

"Thanks Norman – I thought you were having me on at first but I was desperate enough to try anything. That's one I owe you!"

Er... um... Howard, if you are reading this... Could I have my tin back please?

After the show you have to line up to meet the Queen. I stood between Ted Ray and Max Bygraves with my knees still knocking. You would think that after the show all the tension would disappear wouldn't you? It does! But the show is not considered to be over until after the Royal Family have left the theatre.

If you haven't already met the Queen, here's a little tip. The protocol is that you do not speak until you are spoken to. When I stood in line, eyes staring forward as in my Army days, Her Majesty suddenly appeared in front of me, her hand extended. I took it and bowed and waited for her to speak. She didn't say anything but neither did she move on. Her face changed a little and I wondered what was going on. It was almost as if she was struggling with something – then she relaxed, beamed a beautiful smile and said, "It's all been so lovely and so happy!"

She had enjoyed the show tremendously and later I learned

that it was quite true – she did struggle to keep a straight face whenever she saw me!

My next *Royal Variety Show* was in 1954, when a ballet routine that was in my show at the Prince Of Wales Theatre was selected as one of the attractions. The sequence was entitled *Romance In Town* and my partner was the super Gillian Moran. The ballet gave me a chance to express another dimension of humour and proved to be a big hit, both in the show at the Prince Of Wales and the *Royal Variety Show*. Just for the record, I was equally as nervous for my second *Royal Variety Show* as I had been for my first. I have now done nine varied *Royal Variety Shows* and I have had my butterflies with me on every occasion. If anyone tells you that he or she is not nervous before such an engagement – they are telling fibs!

The 1958 *Royal Variety Show* included scenes from *Where's Charley*, in which I was appearing at the time. It gave me a hat-trick of *Royal Variety Shows* in seven years. Two years later I was back again. The 1960 show was the first to be televised. The venue was the Victoria Palace this time and, since there was such an association between that theatre and the Crazy Gang, it seemed appropriate that it included sketches that were entitled, 'Stolen From The Crazy Gang'. I was involved in some of these sketches along with such stars as Benny Hill, Frankie Howerd, Bob Monkhouse, Jimmy Edwards, Diana Dors and Hattie Jacques.

My last *Royal Variety Show* was in 1985, although I did a *Children's Royal Variety Show* in 1988. Perhaps they will ask me back one day. It is certainly a great experience as well as being a very special honour.

The show is not just a big bash for the Royal Family and an ego-booster for all those taking part. It also does a great deal of good as a fund-raiser. In some ways it is a great pity that the cameras are unable to go backstage before the show and while it is running. If you ever want to see absolute chaos at its most hyperactive – grown men and women living in abject fear –

tears, relief and pure insanity – then backstage during a *Royal Variety Show* is the place to be. I have seen people rushing to be sick just before they're due on stage, I have seen them visiting the loo more times in an hour than seems humanly possible and I have seen them reduced to tears with nervous tension before the show, and tears of relief and happiness afterward. Several careers have been launched on the basis of show-stopping performances in the *Royal Variety Show* – and one or two have come close to foundering when the act has not gone as well as was expected. Things can always go wrong of course. There have been costumes split at the worst possible moment and microphones that cease to work just as the comedian delivers his punch-line.

But that's the magic of such a show! If it is live then anything can happen – and probably will – and the *Royal Variety Show* is certainly a live show. It is vibrant, it is exciting, it is frightening, it is SHOWBUSINESS!

In recent years I believe that the show has suffered just a little because of the emphasis on actors and pop groups. I do not say this in any way to denigrate the performances of any of the fine artistes who have been involved in the show but, when you take away the excerpts from this or that musical, scenes from TV soap operas, and appearances by groups who are at their best in major pop concerts, then there is not a lot left!

The *Royal Variety Show* was designed to be just that – a variety show! The appearances by comedians, singers and dancers who are used to a variety type of performance are noticeably more slick than other aspects of the show. Where are the speciality acts – the ventriloquists, the magicians the circus acts? That is what variety is all about and I can't help but think that the *Royal Variety Show* would do variety a big favour by using more acts of that kind. It would be a great incentive for other theatres to follow suit and that would be good news for all those talented people in this country who are finding it harder and harder to get a chance to show what they can do on any sort of stage!

The *Royal Variety Show* raises money for the Variety Artistes Benevolent Fund. It helps to finance Brinsworth House which is the retirement home for entertainers. I often visit Brinsworth House. Josie Leslie lives there; she is the widow of my old pal Eddie Leslie and I like to have a chat with her – as well as everyone else in that lovely house. There is an amazing wealth of talent and experience under that roof – the limbs may be a little tired now, but the hearts are as young and vibrant as ever.

If by any chance you happen to visit Brinsworth House, don't forget to ask to see the Norman Wisdom Room – it is one of the most important rooms in the place, even though I've said it myself! I was flushed with pride when I unveiled it – after all, it IS a toilet! Yes, the Norman Wisdom Room is actually a lavatory – I told you that it was one of the most important rooms in Brinsworth House!

I have told you about my appearances before royalty in the *Royal Variety Shows* – I mentioned that Princess Margaret came to see the ice-show at the Empress Hall – and I have also told you about the Christmas shows at Windsor Castle which I have done several times. That, however, is not the sum total of my royal engagements because I had a very special appointment in 1995 – and that one was at Buckingham Palace!

In the Queen's Birthday Honours List of 1995 I was presented with an OBE – the Order of the British Empire. I really cannot put into words what that means to me because it was such an emotional moment when Her Majesty presented me with it! You see, I have always loved Great Britain and I was never more proud than when I served my country when I was in the Army.

I am not one of those who believe that we are better than foreigners at everything but I am proud of my British heritage and I dearly love the actual land. You can go to any beauty spot in the world and have your breath taken away by the natural splendour that you see – but sometimes we forget about the natural beauty of the British Isles. The White Cliffs of Dover, the Yorkshire Dales, the Cairngorms, the mountains and valleys of

Scotland, Wales, Ireland and the Isle of Man... all too wonderful for words!

So, with the love that I feel for my country, when my country and my Queen bestowed upon me the OBE, I was as delighted as I could possibly be. Her Majesty smiled and said a few words and I could have skipped all the way out of Buckingham Palace. To be honest – we did have a bit of a family celebration afterward!

My OBE is kept in a very secure place and I take it out just to look at it now and then! Call me a silly old so-and-so but it brings tears to my eyes every time that I look at it!

That just about covers my stories of my meetings with the Royal Family except for one thing. Among my souvenirs is a photograph I had taken at Windsor Castle during one of my staff party engagements. A friend took it while I was having a sneaky sit on one of the thrones! There! That's spilled the beans and now I shall probably be asked for the OBE to be returned!... Oh well!... It was good while it lasted!

Back To The Pictures

AFTER the success of *Trouble In Store*, Rank were pretty keen to get the next film into production. It was to be called *One Good Turn* and had a story-line that was very close to my heart. The same production team was called in and the cast included Thora Hird, Shirley Abicair and William Russell.

In the film I am a handyman at an orphanage. I was an orphan there myself and had stayed on after I had grown up. The future of the orphanage is threatened by developers and the film goes on to show the battle to keep it open so that the kids – and Norman – have a place that they can call 'home'. At the same time there is a parallel plot because I – Norman, that is – promise a little lad called Jimmy that I will buy him a super pedal-car. It is for sale at £12 and Norman tries all sorts of things to raise the necessary cash.

I liked the story very much because I could relate to the orphanage. I had never been an orphan myself but I had sometimes felt like one. I also understood how it felt to have your heart really set on something only to see it fading away before your eyes. There is one particular incident in the film that I was also able to play from personal experience. As part of the effort to raise cash for the pedal-car, Norman visits a fairground and tries his hand in the boxing-booth. It reminded me of my evening in a similar situation in far-off Argentina.

I enjoyed the boxing scene. I did a bit of straight boxing and then some comedy stuff and had the time of my life. There was another incident in the film when I got hit by a hard jet of water which lifted me high in the air by the force of the blast. It looked a sensational stunt and got a tremendous laugh. I was actually put into a harness for this and was hoisted into the air by means of a crane when the jet of water hit me.

Another stunt was for the latter part of the film. I finally manage to get the pedal-car, but then I have to get in it and drive it, as fast as I possibly can, under and through miscellaneous obstacles. At one stage I had had to pedal furiously through a large pipe which was a bit like a tunnel. When we were filming it I failed to keep the car exactly straight and it tipped over. I was pitched out and slid the rest of the way along the tunnel with the pedal-car somersaulting along behind me. When we finally came to a stop, I just lay there – out for the count!

Paddy Carstairs was the first to get to me and I was vaguely aware of him loosening my collar and shouting orders at people to get a doctor and an ambulance. I didn't move a muscle or even flicker an eyelid. Paddy was getting more and more worried – close to panic even – and I was unable to keep it up. My face began to crack and I started to laugh. The penny dropped and Paddy realised that I had been having him on again. He fetched me a heck of a wallop and warned me never to pull a stunt like that again. As he walked away I heard him chuckle and so I knew that we hadn't really fallen out. The next time that I thought of winding him up I remembered that fourpenny one and restricted my practical jokes to those which were likely to carry a less painful retribution!

One Good Turn was released in 1954 and, once again, we had a success on our hands. What was much more important to me was that I was learning more about the trade, and I still maintain that, no matter how old you are or how many films you may have made, there is still something new to learn every single day. By keeping that attitude of learning something new every day you can build up quite an education!

Rank were obviously thrilled to bits that our first two ventures had been so successful. They made good profits from the films and were eating away at their previous misfortunes. Plans were already afoot for my next film which was to be called *Man Of The Moment*. There was a slight departure in this production in that Hugh Stewart took over from Maurice Cowan as producer – although the story-line was by Maurice.

In addition to this film, 1955 also saw me playing a very small part in the finale of *As Long As They're Happy*, which starred Jack Buchanan. It also had other star names such as Janette Scott, Diana Dors, Joan Sims, Nigel Green, Joan Hickson, Richard Wattis, Jerry Wayne, Sam Kydd and Hattie Jacques. I appeared right at the end, singing *Don't Laugh At Me*. It was just a bit of fun!

The *Man Of The Moment* film was something different again. The storyline had Norman working as a filing clerk in the Ministry for Overseas Development. When some of the senior members of the staff fall ill, Norman has to be included in the British delegation that goes to Geneva. When one of them has an accident, Norm finds himself in the debating chamber to make up the numbers – although he has strict instructions not to say anything.

When Norman spots his favourite actress watching the debate he waves to her and, by doing so, unwittingly vetoes a resolution concerning the Pacific Islands of Tawakia. This divorces him from his British superiors but endears him to the Tawakian Queen, who considers him to be her country's protector and advisor. In turn, this means that Norman becomes the subject of a lot of creeping and crawling by delegates from all the major powers. He has all kinds of honours bestowed upon him – including a knighthood!

Norman remains essentially the same simple filing clerk who

is looked down on by everyone else but, now they have to accept him and go along with his requirements. It was a lot of fun to make. Lana Morris, Belinda Lee, Jerry Desmonde and Charles Hawtrey were among the stars and there were special guest appearances by a number of television personalities. I wonder how well you remember these? There were – Philip Harben, Ronnie Waldman, McDonald Hobley, The Grove Family and Fabian of the Yard. I sang *Beware*, which I had written in 1951 and always featured in my stage act. The title song was performed by the Beverley Sisters.

Once again the critics were kind and the box-office returns brought big smiles, and even bigger cigars, to the faces of the Rank executives.

Filming at Pinewood was great!

A place like Pinewood is a maze of studios and sets. Usually there are a number of films being shot at the same time and so you bump into all kinds of people that you would never normally meet. You visit their sets and they visit yours – it's surprising how many new friends you make.

As well as the studio sets, different areas are used for vastly different scenes. There is one pillared entrance that has been used for both a mansion and a hospital. One day you could see an ambulance pull up outside to deliver an accident victim, the next it might be a salesman knocking on the door of someone's residence. The following day a vicar could be welcoming wor- shippers to his church while the day after a coach and horses may be drawing up to deliver people to a night at the opera. Same door! Same pillars! Same steps! Only the theme and the camera angle are different – that's the illusion of cinema!

In 1956, *Up In The World* was released and many people say that it was one of the best. I don't know about that myself because I just can't pick a favourite. I really enjoyed every single film that I did. There is one sequence in the film in which I end up as a volunteer from the audience for a magician – which reminded me of my work with David Nixon.

The story is that Norman is a window-cleaner who lands a job at Banderville Park, country home of Sir Reginald, who is actually a young lad under the guardianship of his mother and two uncles, Maurice and Fletcher. Sir Reginald is a compulsive practical joker who finds a great foil in Norman. His mother believes that there is a danger that he might be kidnapped and, as it turns out, she is right! Sir Reginald convinces Norman to take him to the White Cockatoo, a night-club where the celebrated magician, DeMilo, is appearing. Behind the scenes, of course, the White Cockatoo is the headquarters of a notorious gang. Norman's situation looks bad when Sir Reginald is kidnapped. He is implicated in the plot and even after the police rescue the junior Sir, Norman is still in trouble because Sir Reginald has been hit on the head and has lost his memory. Norman is sent to jail but he escapes to try and prove his innocence. In the mêlée which follows, Sir Reginald gets another whack on the bonce and is able to put Norman in the clear. And, of course, lucky Norm gets to marry the girl of his dreams – Jeannie the parlour maid!

Maureen Swanson was Jeannie and also in the cast was Jerry Desmonde, Michael Ward, Eddie Leslie, Lionel Jeffries and many others.

I must have come *Up In The World* with this film because even *The Times* gave us a nice write-up: 'Mr Wisdom seems to have grown in screen self-confidence and the humour, or artless pantomime season, slapdash affair of hit-and-miss, runs up a reasonable score of unambitious, unsophisticated hits.'

I think that was a good write-up!

We were back to Pinewood again for the 1957 film *Just My Luck*. I played both me and my dad. Jill Dixon was in the cast again and among others were Leslie Phillips, Joan Sims, Jerry Desmonde, Eddie Leslie, Michael Ward, Cyril Chamberlain, Bill Fraser, Sam Kydd and dear old Margaret Rutherford. Edward Chapman also joined us and was another great straightman and there was also a part for Vic Wise, in whose TV show I had appeared many times.

Once again Norman is trying to get some money together. He wants to buy a piece of jewellery for Anne, who works as a window-dresser and who has captured the heart of little Norm. Norman's adventures in trying to get the cash involve horse-racing and this gave me the chance to work with horses. A lot of people don't like to work on screen with animals – but it has never bothered me. I suppose that it is easier if you are a comedy entertainer because it doesn't matter if the talented beast makes a fool of you. If you are a serious actor in a scene of high drama it must be extremely difficult to maintain the mood if you are being up-staged in some way by an animal in the scene.

I have worked with animals many times and I have never had a bad experience – although I came close to it when I was having a photo-session with an enormous orang-utan called Spike! When I say that he was enormous, I mean eNORMous! Now orangs are reputed to be normally docile but, I understand, the day after that photo-session he went a bit crazy and killed his handler. I confess to feeling a bit uneasy when I posed with Spike – especially after being warned that he was a little unpredictable! For a long time after that I experienced bad dreams about Spike!

In 1958 *The Square Peg* was released and this was quite a milestone in my cinema career. Sadly it was the last one that I did with Paddy Carstairs. Happily, I became more involved with the scripting and it was this film which saw the birth of Norman Pitkin – the character who was to become internationally famous. Edward Chapman was with us again and became Mr Grimsdale for the first time. Honor Blackman, Hattie Jacques, Terence Alexander, Eddie Leslie and Frank Williams were among the other stars.

The story is about road-digger, Norman Pitkin, getting called up into the Army, along with his St Godric's Borough Council boss, Mr Grimsdale. They soon find themselves at the French front. Grimsdale is taken prisoner but it's Norman to the rescue when it is discovered that he and the local German general are lookalikes. As a reward for his bravery Norman receives the highest award that he can imagine – being made Mayor of St Godric's Borough Council.

It was fellow script-writer, Jack Davies, who came up with the idea of me playing both Norman and the German general. Paddy Carstairs was dead set against the idea at first but he had to go along with it. Paddy had serious doubts about my being able to play the German general straight – but producer Hugh Stewart over-ruled him.

The first time that we did a scene with me as the general, Paddy was in a rare old mood. He was still far from convinced that I could do it. We gave it a try. It went well – or so I thought! Hugh Stewart was watching and gave me a nod of encouragement. Paddy stalked over to me, his face drawn and strained. Then he threw his arms around me and gave me a big kiss on the cheek as if I'd just scored the winning goal in the FA Cup Final. We were pals again and it was Paddy's way of apologising for having doubted my ability.

After *The Square Peg*, Paddy wanted to return to making thrillers for television. We never did work together again and sadly Paddy Carstairs fell ill in 1970 and passed away.

The opening scene in *The Square Peg* was my idea. Outside the Army barracks, Norman Pitkin is doing what he always does best – digging a hole in the road. It is already quite deep but he is still digging away when he hears orders being barked out on the parade ground. His mischievous sense of humour gets the better of him and he barks out an order himself and then ducks below road level so that he cannot be seen. To his delight, the soldiers on parade respond to his order and so he has another go – and thus begins a sequence of turmoil as the men respond to orders, first from the sergeant-major and then from Pitkin. It works beautifully and is often requested in television programmes showing favourite clips. I am very proud of that.

Robert Asher took over from Paddy Carstairs for what was the last of seven films which I had been contracted to make for Rank, *Follow A Star*. Robert had been first assistant on *One Good Turn* and *Man Of The Moment*. We had a busy cast list again including June Laverick, Jerry Desmonde, Hattie Jacques, Richard Wattis, Eddie Leslie, John Le Mesurier, Fenella Fielding, Joe Melia, Richard Caldicott, Ron Moody, Dick Emery, Sydney Tafler and Charles Gray. Quite a list, eh?

Do you remember my last night of the *Let's Make Hay* tour? When I was told that I would never work again at the Metropolitan, Edgware Road! Well, ironically, I went back there for some of the filming for *Follow A Star*. The story was about Norman Trustcott – me again – who is an assistant at a cleaners. His hero, Vernon Carew, comes to the establishment to have a suit cleaned and is spotted by Norman. In return for his adulation, Norman is given two free tickets for a performance by Carew.

The show is poorly attended and Vernon Carew is going down like a lead balloon. Norman wants to help and so he encourages the audience to join in and sing. Carew hears his voice and hatches a plot to relaunch his own flagging career. As a result of recording Norman's voice, Carew gets into the charts. The plot thickens and culminates in Carew – and Norman – appearing at the London Palladium, where the villainous Vernon is exposed and little Norm becomes a star.

Once again the film was a success and the *Daily Express* was particularly kind: 'Norman Wisdom's best film yet! The little man just fools around, being funny in his own inimitable way and demonstrating once more why he is the only star in British films today who has consistently made a profit for the Rank organisation.'

It was time for renewed negotiations with Rank and we finally agreed that we would henceforth operate on a film by film basis – and it was on this understanding that we shot *The Bulldog Breed*, for release in 1960. Now this was a particularly interesting film because the cast included two 'new boys' who, I believe, have gone on to great careers. I don't know if you have ever heard of them since – one answers to the name of Oliver Reed and the other is a bloke called Michael Caine. They were both in *The Bulldog Breed*, but not many people know that!

Also among the cast were Ian Hunter, David Lodge, Robert Urquhart, Edward Chapman, Eddie Byrne, Peter Jones, Terence Alexander, John Le Mesurier, Sydney Tafler, Liz Fraser, Penny Morrell, Harold Goodwin, Johnny Briggs, Leonard Sachs, Glyn Houston and Sheila Hancock.

I am Norman Puckle, a delivery boy with Dalton's Yacht Service. I propose to a girl cashier at the local cinema who turns me down. I decide to end it all but I even fail at that. The Navy rescues me after one attempt and that opens up a new career since I decide to become a new recruit. I end up looking after the admiral's bulldog, Bosun, who gets loose and chases a rabbit into a Navy test rocket. I try to get him out and the inevitable happens. The rocket is launched and eventually lands me on a Polynesian Island, where I find paradise in the arms of a beautiful native girl. No, I didn't write the script – well, not all of it!

It was a winner again and Rank were happy to talk about another film but, in the meantime, I had signed an additional contract with Knightsbridge Films, which was owned by John Bryan and Ronald Neame. My first film for them was called *There Was A Crooked Man*, and among the stars were Alfred Marks, Andrew Cruikshank, Susannah York, Glyn Houston, Jack May, Ronald Fraser, Ed Devereaux and Sam Kydd.

This was also filmed at Pinewood Studios and my role as Davy Cooper was slightly different. I was out of the Gump suit and into something a little more respectable. The film owed more to farce than to slapstick and I enjoyed making it. The box-office was good and it was decided to do another.

Once again I had a very different character to play in *The Girl On The Boat*. I was Sam Marlowe, a well-off layabout – not unlike P.G.Wodehouse's famous Bertie Wooster. Once again there was a strong cast assembled, including Millicent Martin, Richard Briers, Sheila Hancock, Bernard Cribbins, Ronald Fraser, Dick Bentley, Timothy Bateson and Peter Bull.

Henry Kaplan was our director, it was his debut film and he has since made a name for himself in television.

The Girl On The Boat did well but it was not as well received as the others that I'd done. For me it was very good to tackle a different character and I accepted the challenge with relish. The film was released in 1962 and in that same year I had another film, *On The Beat*, released by Rank.

Hugh Stewart was the producer again and, for me, it was a return to the character of Norman Pitkin. I was on the scripting team along with Eddie Leslie and Jack Davies. Once again I had two parts to play since I was also the arch-villain, Giulio Napolitani. Among the others were Jennifer Jayne, Raymond Huntley, David Lodge, Esma Cannon, Eric Barker, Eleanor Summerfield, Terence Alexander, Maurice Kaufmann, Dilys Laye, Lionel Murton, Alfred Burke and John Blythe.

The storyline is all about Norman Pitkin's desire to be a policeman like his dad had been. There is one small problem – Norman is about a foot too short! Norman gets a job at the police station but it is just to wash the cars – and even that results in the sack. It is discovered that Norman bears quite a resemblance to one of the underworld's chief crooks, Giulio Napolitani, who runs his shady business from the back of his high-class ladies' hairdressers. Norman is recruited and finally, of course, Giulio meets his match when PC Pitkin makes pasta out of him!

There are a number of reasons why this film sticks in my mind. One is a scene with Eric Barker in which I am supposed to be having a medical to see if I am suitable to become a policeman. I actually don a pair of stilts to increase my height. Although we had roughly worked out what would happen, most of the details in this scene were quite ad-lib and the end result is quite hilarious, thanks to the brilliant improvisation by Eric Barker.

In another scene I am being taught how to walk like Napolitani, who has a rather effeminate style that is all his own. There was a lot of larking about in this scene but it worked very well. We had a problem with another scene in which I am wearing my dad's old police uniform, which is not only out of date but also several sizes too big for me. David Lodge was the problem! He was playing Superintendent Hobson and we had to play a lot of scenes together. David has a great sense of humour and when he saw me in the outsize uniform he just couldn't control himself and collapsed in laughter. It took a lot of takes to complete that particular scene and, even then, it was only completed to director Bob Asher's satisfaction after he had moved me out of sight while David did his lines.

Once again Rank had a box-office success and they followed it a year later with *A Stitch In Time*. This time Norman Pitkin was seeking help from his boss, Mr Grimsdale. There was another large cast for this 1963 film with Edward Chapman, Jeanette Sterke, Jerry Desmonde, Glyn Houston, Patsy Rowlands, Peter Jones, Frank Williams, Patrick Cargill, Francis Matthews, Johnny Briggs and John Blythe, among others.

Jack Davies wrote the original story and then we talked about it. I made a lot of suggestions which would be written in. Eventually he said that he thought it was unfair that I didn't get a credit – so my name went up as well. Eddie Leslie was also a good writer and it got so that Jack didn't mind as long as we'd finish it. Eventually, Eddie and I went off to Spain and wrote the entire script, just from Jack's notes and those pencilled in ideas – and we put his name to it! But Jack was good and always wanted to be fair to everyone concerned – a marvellous bloke!

Mr Grimsdale is a respectable butcher and Norman Pitkin is his assistant. Life starts to go wrong when there is a hold-up at the shop. Mr Grimsdale swallows his watch and chain and has to go to hospital. While visiting him, Norman also meets a recently orphaned little girl named Lindy. Norman tries to cheer her up and he also hears of a special fund-raising effort in aid of a children's holiday home appeal. Norman wants to help and, naturally enough, the chaos ensues.

The film called for one fantastic sequence which I dearly wanted to do myself. Unfortunately, Bob Asher would not hear of it and insisted on using a stuntman. It starts off with Norman, bandaged from head to toe and in plaster, attempting to get into a wheelchair so that he can go and watch a game of football. When he gets into the wheelchair it takes off and he bumps his way down a flight of stairs before crashing through a wall. At that moment an ambulance is passing by. Norman lands on its roof and hangs on until it throws him off at a sharp corner. Norman is propelled through a glass window into a hospital ward, whereupon he slides along the polished floor until he crashes into the wall at the far end of the ward. A doctor, played superbly by Patrick Cargill, looks down at Norman and says, "Nurse, what is this patient doing out of bed?"

I was really disappointed when Bob told me about the stuntman. I went to watch the sequence being filmed and couldn't believe my eyes when the stuntman slipped off the ambulance roof and broke his arm. A dismayed Bob Asher was in a real spot because he didn't want to lose the day's filming. I volunteered to do the scene myself and, after a bit of persuasion, he reluctantly agreed. By the end of the day we had the whole thing in the can!

Next time you see *A Stitch In Time*, take a close look at that sequence. I promise you that the entire stunt was performed by me!

A Stitch In Time broke box-office records all over London and the provinces. It actually took more money than the high-profile release, starring Sean Connery as James Bond, *From Russia With Love*!

Two years after that success, I became Norman Pitkin again in another Rank production – *The Early Bird*. This time Mr Grimsdale is running a dairy with Norman as his milkman. All is going fine until the all-conquering Consolidated Dairies move into the neighbourhood and try to put Grimsdale out of business. Even when Mr Grimsdale is prepared to capitulate, Norman is determined not to stand by and just watch it end. He is prepared to fight to the last homogenised drop!

Edward Chapman was Mr Grimsdale again and there were

such names as Jerry Desmonde, Paddie O'Neal, Bryan Pringle, Richard Vernon, John Le Mesurier, Peter Jeffrey, Frank Thornton, Imogen Hassall, Dandy Nichols, Michael Bilton, Eddie Leslie and David Lodge.

The box-office brought another smile to the Rank Organisation but there was some disagreement about the next film. Rank wanted to continue with the same arrangement but I wanted to be able to have some greater 'say' in the film content. Rank did not want that and so we pulled faces at each other for a while before reaching further agreement.

In 1966 we had another Rank film at the pictures. I also had a nine-minute role to play in *The Sandwich Man*. I was an eccentric priest! Michael Bentine was the main comic and there were enough stars in support to fill a 'Who's Who'!

The Rank film was *Press For Time*, in which I was Norman Shields, a newspaper seller who is grandson to the Prime Minister. Through his famous grandad, Norman lands a job as a newspaper reporter for a local rag on the coast – with all the expected results.

Journalists who have chatted to me say that they have all met a 'Norman Shields' and found some of his adventures to be hilarious. I hope so because it was such fun to do. Derek Bond, Angela Browne, Tracey Crisp, Peter Jones, David Lodge, Stanley Unwin and Gordon Rollings were among those in the cast.

The sad point about this film was that it was the last for Bob Asher. He went to television for a while but then did very little for some years. He eventually died in 1979 – a great loss of talent.

In 1969 I was associate producer, script-writer and star in *What's Good For The Goose*. It was a Tigon film, directed by Menahem Golan, who went on to become a big name in the film and television industry. Sally Geeson, Terence Alexander and David Lodge were among the many names in the cast. To be honest, this was not one of the best films. It had its moments but it did not compare with the others.

Having taken the trip to America, as I previously told you, I found that the film industry had changed, seemingly overnight, when we returned. The investment and demand for the sort of films that we had been creating had disappeared. That doesn't mean that there was a shortage of work for me. Even though there was a lull in the film industry, I continued with my theatre tours, summer seasons and pantos. I hope it doesn't sound as if I'm blowing my own trumpet when I say that we broke quite a few box-office records around this time too.

There was also television with its shows and its commercials. I was still a useful commodity. Rank had turned their deficit into profit with the help of my films and I had made a lot of mates – generally known as 'the public' – and so I was able to continue doing what I have always done – entertain my friends. I'm happy to say that from those very early days of living on my wits until now, I have never been out of work. I do feel for those who have – and who are now – and I'd simply like to say – NEVER GIVE UP!

Television gave me a wonderful opportunity to appear in *Going Gently*. I was invited to the Television Centre near Shepherd's Bush to have lunch with Innes Lloyd and Stephen Frears. It was Innes who had made the initial approach to Billy Marsh to see if I might be interested in a very serious straight role. Stephen was the director.

The story was about Bernard Flood, a man in hospital dying from cancer. Fulton Mackay was to be a fellow patient in the next bed and among the others in the cast was Judi Dench as Sister Scarli, and Stephanie Cole as Gladys Flood. The production was for that excellent BBC series *Playhouse*.

It was a very delicate subject and would call for some hard work if the public were to forget about Norman and concentrate on poor Bernard, the cancer victim. I was well aware of what was required.

After that lunch, Stephen Frears asked me to come to his office for a further chat. He explained to me that there was no room for humour in the play and I could sense that he didn't really think that I was up to the role.

"Oh, I wouldn't say that there are no opportunities for humour. Imagine if I was wearing a hospital gown and got out of bed, only to catch it on a bed-spring – then, as it pulled me back on to the bed, I catch my foot in the chamberpot. That would have got a laugh wouldn't it?"

As I spoke his face went red until, finally, he told me that there was to be no humour whatsoever.

Now it was my turn to hit the roof. I stood up and yelled at him: "Why the hell did you send for me? Wasting my time! I don't have to be messed about by the likes of you, you know! It's a flaming liberty!"

Stephen was really taken aback.

"Please Norman, calm down, calm down," he tried to pacify me.

I grinned at him. "I am calm – but how was that for acting?"

He smiled back at me, shook my hand and said, "Okay Norman! I take your point – the part is yours!"

It was an almost eerie experience to play that part, but there was a wonderful team both in front and behind the cameras. We all became emotionally involved with the cancer victims and, after one particular scene, everyone had tears in their eyes.

Before doing that play I used to smoke cigarettes and have the occasional cigar – I haven't touched either since.

Going Gently was a tremendous success and, I understand, it had quite a profound effect on the nation. This was shown by the many heart-rending letters and phone-calls that the BBC received from those who had lost loved-ones in similar circumstances. I don't know if any of them were helped by the play but I think that it might have eased their pain just a little by knowing that they are not alone in their experience. My television work became much more varied after that. I was still called upon to trip over my own feet on variety shows – but there were also other roles such as playing a safe-cracker in *Bergerac*.

Then, in June 1992, I was back on the big screen again in a film called *Double X*. I am a gangster in the film – not a very nice person at all. William Katt and Gemma Craven were among the others and we enjoyed filming it. As a villain, several attempts were made on my life, and that involved some stunts, which again I was able to do myself. Once you know how to fall, you can always do it – which is why, in some parts of the Orient, you can still get fellows of about two hundred years old teaching judo!

Probably *Double X* could have been better, but it wasn't bad and enjoyed a moderate success at the box-office. It will probably turn up on television one of these days. Can't keep away from television for very long, can we? In September 1994, I spent a wonderful week or so in Yorkshire, filming for that terrific comedy programme, *Last Of The Summer Wine*.

It is one of my favourite programmes and when I was asked to appear in what was basically the 1994 Christmas Special, I was very excited. When I read the part, I had no hesitation in accepting it.

The area in which we were filming the location scenes is absolutely beautiful and, if you haven't already been to the Holmfirth area of Yorkshire, I would urge you to treat yourself to a lovely part of England.

I had to play the part of a bit of a nutcase who had always wanted to be a concert pianist. Filming with Brian Wilde, Bill Owen and Peter Sallis was great fun and made the job very easy – then, with such a marvellous cast list as Thora Hird, Kathy Staff, Jean Ferguson, Stephen Lewis and the others, the atmosphere throughout the filming was thoroughly enjoyable. I'm told that the episode was well received and, who knows, perhaps I'll be asked again some time?

I am not finished with the film industry yet. For some time I have owned the script of a potential film called *Adam And Evil*. It is based on a J.B.Priestley story and tells the tale of a lonely musician who yearns to have a lady in his life. He ends up with a kind of genie who turns out to be his ideal woman. The only problem is that she turns out to be the boss and he has a big problem trying to get her out of his life. The film is scheduled for production before the end of 1996 – and I am the lonely musician. It promises to be another new challenge and one that I shall certainly relish. It's good to be going back to the pictures again!

Two Gumps together!

Left: **A new hat for David Nixon.**

Above: **Having a laugh with Harry Secombe.**

Right: **Dick Emery was also an old mate.**

Above: Playing 'I-Spy'
with Sean Connery.

Left: This was on
the front of the *New
York Times*.

Left: Keeping up with the Mills. Here are Mr and Mrs John Mills and their daughter Hayley.

Right: Voted Britain's Top Comedian in 1964. That's Lord and Lady Delfont with my wife, Freda, on the right.

Above: The fourth member of the Beverley Sisters – my Mum!

Left: 'Smudger' Smith!

Next page, bottom left: With my daughter Jacqui and son Nicky at a family party.

Above: I nicked one of Britt Ekland's sandwiches.

Bottom right: He was 7ft 5½ins and weighed 29 stone, and he wanted his picture taken with me… I didn't argue!

Top left: I joined the Red Army in Moscow.

Top right: A Clowns International Convention.

Centre: "You little tinker!"

Bottom left: Those are my 'wheels'.

Bottom right: "Nice to see you again, Your Majesty!"

Left: I bumped into Rod and Elton at the 1983 Cup Final when Brighton played Manchester United.

Right: Jack Charlton was there too.

Left: Tony Fayne bossing me about again.

Left: I can't
resist horses.

Above: "Know what
I mean Norm?"

Right: 'The Early
Bird' on tour in
Edinburgh in 1993.

Above: Brian Wilde, Peter Sallis and Bill Owen and yours truly in *Last of the Summer Wine*.

Left: Filming in *Last of the Summer Wine*.

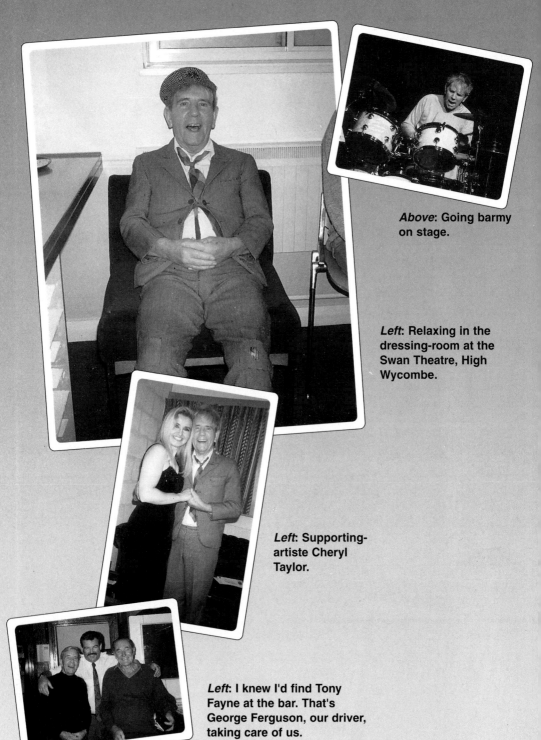

Above: Going barmy on stage.

Left: Relaxing in the dressing-room at the Swan Theatre, High Wycombe.

Left: Supporting-artiste Cheryl Taylor.

Left: I knew I'd find Tony Fayne at the bar. That's George Ferguson, our driver, taking care of us.

Left: Our guards in Tirana, Albania.

Right: Pat Dickenson, Johnny Mans, me and Jimmy Noon on our Albanian trip.

Bottom left: Sliding into an Albanian orphanage.

Bottom right: A newspaper 'special edition' in Albania.

'COS I'M A FOOL

Top left: BBC TV Producer, Alan J.Bell, congratulates me on my 'Freedom of the City of London'.

Top right: I decide to become an agent.

VE celebrations in Canterbury in 1995.

Above: With Dame Vera Lynn meeting the Duchess of Kent at St James' Palace.

Centre left: Comparing ties with Terry Waite.

Centre right: Sue Nicholls from *Coronation Street* shows me a few new dance steps.

Top right: Bumping into Michael Foot at the BBC.

Left: Fore? There's more than four Ping clubs in 'ere mate!

Top left: Showing grandson Lawrence my OBE.

Top right: You should have seen the other bloke!

Centre left: Filming a Sanyo commercial.

Centre right: That was my bedroom when I was a kid in Paddington.

Bottom: Welcome to Ballalaugh.

The press launch for *Adam and Evil*.

That's me today... You should see your faces!

Today's Tours

IN THE autumn of 1996 I will be on the road again for nearly two months, travelling from town to town to appear at theatres in various parts of Britain. I am not going to pretend that it is not hard work because it most definitely is, but then, it has always been hard work – not just for me, but for everyone! If anyone finds it easy then they must be doing it wrong.

Perhaps you would like to travel with us on a typical tour to see what life is like on the road. The preparations begin many months, if not a whole year, in advance and that is where my agent, Johnny Mans, comes in. John was with Billy Marsh for some years and took over when Billy finally retired. I have known him for a good many years now and we talk to each other most days because there is always some new proposition coming in – perhaps a live appearance, a TV commercial, a cruise or whatever.

We generally schedule a year to eighteen months ahead and section off different periods for different activities. In 1996 we have given over about two months of the late autumn for a tour. Even this is subject to change because the film schedule for *Adam And Evil* could possibly make a difference. But in general, once a tour period has been set, John can get on with arranging actual dates for the respective theatres.

That date arranging is not as easy as it sounds because there is so much to be taken into consideration. When were we last there? What dates are currently available at the theatre? Is the available date a good one, or does it clash with some other major event in the town? How soon after some other comedy show will we be appearing? How does the proposed date fit in with the rest of the tour? – You wouldn't want dates that send you to Glasgow on Monday, Plymouth on Tuesday and then up to Edinburgh on Wednesday! The dates need to 'gel' together in a sensible way.

When a date has been finally agreed, the financial arrangements have to be decided. When that stage has been completed to the satisfaction of both parties, the theatre will be asked how many posters and handbills are required and these will then be ordered from the printer. Newspaper advertising is discussed, the press agent is informed and the wheels are set in motion to ensure, as much as possible, that everyone knows we are coming to town.

All that and we haven't even started yet! Once the dates are organised the support programme is engaged. I always do the second half – but we need a good audience-pleasing first half as well! I like to have a quality singer, some comedy, and perhaps a speciality act if at all possible. If you have a good first half, it not only builds up the mood in the theatre, but it also gives the public a value-for-money show. That support programme also includes the musicians and we have to make sure that they are all available.

So we now have our dates and our show! Next the hotels and the transport have to be organised. We generally have a coach for the entire party as we prefer to travel together. You might think that now we have all that sorted out we are, at last, home and dry – but it's not quite as easy as that! There is always a great demand for press, radio and television interviews during the tour and I also like to try and get some time to myself to visit friends – and the occasional car showroom.

Before the tour proper begins we need to have some rehearsal time although, for me, since my work includes the whole of the second half, I no longer have need to rehearse sketches and other routines as I did in years gone by. As long as the musical director, Terry White, knows what we are doing – and my long-time straight man, Tony Fayne, and I are on the same wavelength – then we are on our way!

A typical tour is like this one – from 1994:

MARCH

Thurs 31st ......   Wyvern Theatre, Swindon.

APRIL

Fri 1st ....   Playhouse Theatre, Weston Super Mare.
Sat 2nd ....   White Rock Theatre, Hastings.
Sun 3rd ....   Prince's Theatre, Clacton.
Mon 4th ....   Royalty Theatre, Great Yarmouth.
Wed 6th ....   Festival Theatre, Paignton.
Thurs 7th ......   Gordon Craig Theatre, Stevenage.
Fri 8th ....   Assembly Hall, Walthamstow.
Sat 9th ....   Harlequin Theatre, Redhill.
Sun 10th ......   Cliffs Pavilion, Southend.
Tues 12th ......   Hotel Burstin, Folkestone.
Wed 13th ......   Apollo, Oxford.
Thurs 14th .....   Prince of Wales, Colwyn Bay.
Fri 15th ....   Derngate Theatre, Northampton.
Sat 16th ....   Royal Spa Theatre, Leamington Spa.
Sun 17th ....   Wycombe Swan, High Wycombe.
Mon 18th ......   Beck Theatre, Hayes.
Wed 20th ......   Marina Theatre, Lowestoft.
Thurs 21st .....   Victoria Theatre, Halifax.
Sat 23rd ......   Marlowe Theatre, Canterbury.
Tue 26th ....   Fairfield Halls, Croydon.

Wed 27th . . . .   Pier Pavilion, Sandown.

Thurs 28th . . . . . .   Worthing Pavilion, Worthing.

MAY

Sun 1st . . . .   Brentwood Centre, Brentwood.

Mon 2nd . . . .   Epsom Playhouse.

Wed 4th . . . .   Theatre Hafren, Newtown.

Thurs 5th . . . .   Hexagon Theatre, Reading.

As you can see, there were nine days with no shows – but these were not necessarily days off since at least one involved a trip to Birmingham for an appearance on BBC's *Pebble Mill*, and there were various other similar engagements. I think that there were actually two days off from the end of March to the end of the tour on 5 May.

The 1996 tour is scheduled for the autumn, but for the last two years we have had spring tours. This usually gives us a fighting chance with the weather. Travelling from town to town on icy roads, through fog or blizzard, is no fun I promise you. Some years we will do both spring and autumn tours but, for the last few years, this has not been possible owing to other commitments.

Taking 1994 as an example, we arrive at Swindon to open our tour at the Wyvern Theatre. We check into our hotel and then drift along to the theatre. Anne Axe is my personal assistant when we are at work and she checks the dressing-rooms and sees that all the arrangements needed for my spot have been met. One of the side issues on tours like this is merchandise. Years ago we never even thought of selling souvenirs. The theatre would sell its own show programme and that was about it. Today, everything is different. People love to collect souvenirs whether they are watching a show, going to a football match, or having a day by the seaside. If we didn't have a selection of CDs, videos, brochures and so on, they would be very disappointed. And now this book, of course!

On the first night we are at the theatre a little earlier than usual and we'll probably grab a light snack before the place opens its doors to the public. I remain in my dressing-room now. I don't like peeping through the curtains at the audience but I do like to hear them on the theatre's intercom system. Often before the show, one or two old friends drop in to say hello – but once the music starts they disappear to watch the performance and I am left alone to make my preparations.

I can hear the show in progress as I slip off my shirt and take a look in the mirror. My goodness Norm! You're a handsome chap! I grin because I know that I'm only kidding myself – but if I don't say it then who will? I wash my face and start to apply my make-up, pausing now and then to pull a face at myself to make sure that it's looking right.

Once I am satisfied that the make-up is as I want it, I stand up and go to the hanging rail. There is my old friend, the Gump suit. On with the shirt and the string tie, on with the trousers, on with the jacket and, finally, on with the cap. Norman Wisdom is now Norman Pitkin – or simply Norm!

Soon it is interval time. Terry White checks in to make sure that everything is all right. Perhaps one of the artistes will call by to tell me something about the audience or the stage. Tony Fayne will look in as well and, before long, the interval is coming to a close. It is time to go to the wings. I take a last look in the mirror.

The music starts and Tony Fayne introduces himself to the audience. He then begins the build-up to my entrance and I can't wait to get out there. My music begins, I take a deep breath and put my head round the curtains. The place erupts. They are friendly! A little bashful, I step out – I take a pace forward and then step back again. I'm not sure that the applause and cheers are for me. I ask with my hands – miming to them, "Do you mean me?... Are you really pleased to see me?... Honestly?" The applause continues – it is for me! "Oh, thank you – I love you too! I think you are wonderful, all my pals!... Let's have some fun together!"

I go to the centre of the stage where Tony Fayne is waiting

with growing impatience. He has that look in his eye – "Maybe they like you… but, to me, you're a nobody!" I want to be friends with him but he won't have it – toffee-nosed so-and-so! Every time I try to do something it goes wrong and throughout my attempts Tony Fayne remains aloof. Even when he offers to teach me rhythm, there is a catch in it.

He brings out on to the stage a contraption which looks as if it might have been rescued from the Spanish Inquisition. It is the prop that Bernard Delfont obtained for me in 1954. It has a seat with a hole in the middle and a wicked-looking paddle with spikes underneath it. Also attached is a drum, a cymbal, a giant hammer and a pole with a boxing glove on it. I'll leave the rest to your own imagination.

During the act I play various musical instruments, get knocked from pillar to post, dance, sing, and generally have a good time for about an hour and twenty minutes. I listen to the laughter to make sure that my mates in the audience are enjoying themselves as much as me.

The time seems to go very quickly when I'm working and before long it is all over. The audience is applauding for the last time that evening and, after a final wave, I make my way back to the dressing-room. I am soaked in sweat but I am still excited and it takes me a while to calm down. I cannot wait around too long though because I know that there will be people waiting to see me and I don't want them missing their buses or to be too late getting home.

A quick shower and I am at the stage door as quickly as I can, ready to sign autographs, shake hands or just chat.

"Hello Norman! You won't remember this, but we met twenty years ago when you were at such-and-such a theatre!"

How often I hear that! I try my best to remember, and I do pride myself on having a good memory for faces, and it is surprising how often I do remember them. Even if I don't, a little prompting usually does the trick. Whether or not I remember, it is always good to talk about past times.

The trouble with meeting people after the show is that I completely lose track of the time – and sometimes Anne has to remind me that the theatre manager is waiting to lock up.

The last handshakes and kisses are exchanged and we make our way back to the hotel. I still need to unwind a little so there will be a cup of tea and a sandwich – maybe half-an-hour in front of the television, or a chat among ourselves before finally turning in.

I have always been an early riser and sometimes I'll go for a walk or a jog before breakfast. There is very little time after breakfast because we are soon piling into the coach for the journey to our next venue. I like to sit up front next to George, our driver. There is a mobile phone so sometimes I do press interviews while we are on the move.

The atmosphere on the coach is a little like a football team on its way to a match. Some like to read, some doze, some play cards and some just chat. Often we chat about past experiences at the town we're heading for – or about the last time that we met someone who came to see us at last night's performance.

As the time approaches one o'clock, we start to look for a suitable lunch spot. Quite often we have been on this same road before and so we dig into our memories of meals of the past. Was there a place just along here where we enjoyed a great meal last year?... I think we had an awful meal down this way two years ago! Maybe it's a place that we haven't visited before but, rest assured, we will have given it our rating by the time we leave!

After lunch we continue on our journey. The coach drops us at our hotel and then goes on to the theatre to unload the props. Later, it will return for us. We check in at the hotel and, if there is nothing else on the agenda, we will rest a bit before going down to the theatre for the show. Very often though, there are things to do. More press interviews are often held at the hotel.

"How long have you been an entertainer, Mr Wisdom?"

"Since December 1945!"

"What was your favourite film, Mr Wisdom?"

"All of them!"

"When are you going to retire, Mr Wisdom?"

"Pass!"

And so it goes on.

I try to catch up with letter-writing during the afternoons as well – and, if I get the chance, I like to have a look around the town in which we are appearing, especially if we are at the seaside. There is nothing like a British seaside resort – a wonderful institution!

Every town has a story to tell. I can remember most audiences from previous visits and, quite often, people bringing their children to see me, tell me that they were at the same age as their children when they first saw me at that same theatre.

I remember a little girl at Skegness who dislocated her jaw because she laughed so much!

There was a couple who celebrated their golden wedding anniversary by coming to see Norman Wisdom and another couple that came straight from their wedding reception to see the show! Sometimes I turn up at a theatre to find a stage-manager, or some other backstage technician, who has been in the business almost as long as I have – that's when we can really swap a few memories!

In the band there is bass player, John Ditchfield. As well as being an excellent musician, John, whom I have known for many years, also acts, on occasions, as company manager on our tours. It is an unenviable task because he has to represent the promoter and sort out any little problem that may arise on the tour. He deserves a special mention because trying to keep us lot in order is no mean feat!

Our 1996 tour will include Southend, Worthing, Norwich, Skegness, York, Northampton, Wimbledon, Nottingham, Dudley, Stevenage, Barnsley, Walthamstow, Leeds, Llandudno, New-town, King's Lynn, Salisbury and Tunbridge Wells. We start in October and will be on the road until late November. It is a typical itinerary and I'm looking forward to it.

Even now, we are talking about a period in 1997 when we can tour again.

Perhaps we shall meet at one of my theatre dates! Don't be shy! Come and say hello. I might not be able to get you all on to our coach but at least we can share a small part of our tour together!

There is nothing quite like travelling from theatre to theatre with a show. The company is like a family and, at the end of every journey, there is a new challenge, a chance to see new faces, and the possibility of meeting up again with old friends.

Lovely!

Albania, Here We Come!

MY TRAVELS have taken me to some unlikely places and to some unusual experiences. Among the more recent are trips to Albania and to one of the most chilling places on earth – Chernobyl! But, before we venture to those places let me take you on a few trips from the past.

In 1965, Eddie Leslie and I travelled to Argentina for the Mar del Plata Film Festival. *A Stitch In Time* was being shown at the festival and I had been invited to attend – Eddie travelling with me for company. It turned out to be quite a trip. While we were there, a local film distributor, by the name of Pablo Corenthes, asked us if we would like to include a brief trip to Chile in our itinerary.

"I could fly you there in my private plane, show you around, stop a night, and then bring you back," he offered.

Eddie and I both fancied flying over the Andes – we might never get the chance again – so we readily agreed. Sure enough, the next day we were treated to some fantastic views of the Andes and we landed safely at Santiago airport. Our new friend, Pablo, had done us proud. We were taken to a wonderful outdoor restaurant, near the hotel where we were to spend the night. Eddie and I were enjoying ourselves and we were given the use of Pablo's car and chauffeur for a couple of hours so that we could see the sights of Santiago.

While we were doing our tourist bit, cars suddenly began swerving all over the road and people on the pavement were reeling about as if they had drunk too much of the local brew. We were rammed by another vehicle, which turned out to be a taxi, and then Eddie and I realised what was happening.

"It's a flaming earthquake!" we chorused.

As we looked out of the car we could see buildings shaking and walls starting to collapse. Our driver told us that it would be safer to leave the vehicle. We didn't need any prompting! There was a large city square and we ran into the centre of it to get as far away as possible from falling debris.

I realised that I had left my camera in the car and I rushed back to get it. I was just about to grab the door handle when our driver yelled out to me. An electricity cable was touching the car and had made it live. If I had touched that door handle I would have gone up in smoke!

The quake passed and we made our way on foot to the hotel, which was still intact but in a bit of disarray. There was no electricity and we had to help ourselves to something to eat — which meant bread and cheese for Eddie and me. We were concerned about after-shocks and spent the whole night counting the hours as neither of us could sleep.

It was not the first time that I had experienced an earthquake. I had fallen off my bike during a tremor in India — but this one had been much more devastating. We learned later that over 400 people had lost their lives during the quake.

Back safely in Buenos Aires, I took Eddie to visit some of the places that I'd seen when I travelled there aboard ship as a lad. Nothing had changed very much!

At the Film Festival I was thrilled to receive the Golden Flame Award, which they gave me as 'The Most Popular Artiste of all

Nations'. There was a tale attached to that because James Mason was also there as a specially invited guest. He was, of course, a wonderful actor and a gentleman – but I think he got a bit carried away with his own self-importance on this occasion.

James felt that, as he was a big international star, he should go on the stage after me, rather than before me as the reception organisers had planned at the Mar del Plata Theatre. Personally, I couldn't have cared less who went where or who did what, so there was no protest from me.

It has always been a policy of mine that, when you are abroad, you should, at least, be able to greet people in their own language. It is often enough just to say "Hello," and "Thank you for inviting me and I'm glad you like my films," – that sort of thing. Well, I had learned to do that in Spanish and, when I was introduced on stage at the Mar del Plata and spoke those few words in Spanish, it brought the place down. Most foreign people take it as a great compliment if you at least TRY to learn their language.

James Mason had made no attempt to learn the language and was greeted by polite applause when he appeared – an embarrassing contrast to the cheers and enthusiastic clapping that I had received only a few minutes earlier.

It costs nothing to have manners – and it can be very rewarding.

Another Film Festival that I attended was in Moscow. There were a number of us Brits there, but also stars like Bob Hope and Peter Ustinov, so you can see that the Moscow Film Festival was quite a spectacular affair. There were a number of cinemas in use and they were showing a season of my films but, when it came to *Trouble In Store*, that was being shown in an 18,000-seater stadium. It was packed, and to hear that many people enjoying your work is a wonderful experience.

The dialogue was dubbed into Russian but nothing appeared to have been lost in the translation and the Russians, who have a great and loud sense of humour, loved the film. At the end of the showing of *Trouble In Store* I went on stage and, in Russian, simply said, "Hello everyone, you are a lovely people – thank you!"

The place erupted and many people stormed the stage. I thought I had said the wrong thing at first – but they just wanted to shake my hand. Fortunately, the security people kept things under control and allowed just a few at a time to come forward.

The Russians have quite a dour image back here in Britain but believe me – they are a very warm and hospitable people who just love to laugh.

Mentioning Bob Hope reminds me that he and I met again in Berlin at yet another Film Festival. By the way, forget about the so-called glamour of these events, they are actually hard work because you are for ever being taken here, there, and everywhere, – to meet the press, attend functions, shake hands with important people and so on! It's good to get back home and be able to take your shoes off!

Film Festivals are also full of surprises – like the reception I received in Moscow. In Berlin, there was a totally different surprise when Bob Hope took the stage. He had been practising my walk and used it to make his entrance!

I am still invited to make special appearances all over the world but some of the places where I am asked to go are problem zones and, much as I would like to go, the situation in these places means that it could be a hazard that would be better avoided.

In Iran, for instance, my films are still being regularly shown. It seems that the Iranians love them and continually request that they be shown on television. You wouldn't think that an Englishman would be so popular in that part of the Middle East would you? I receive letters all the time and requests for signed photographs – I always oblige!

I have been to Iran in the past. It was in 1974 when the country was still under the rule of the Shah. Tony Fayne was with me and we did a special show for the Shah and his family and friends at the Palace. There were about three hundred people there and we performed in a huge, opulent banqueting hall. After the show we met the Shah and he struck me as being a very pleasant man who wanted his country to enjoy the same freedom that the West enjoyed. His wife, Empress Farah Dibah, was a striking lady – not only very attractive but well over six feet tall. They were a nice family.

While in Teheran, we were also booked into a place called the Sheka Fah Nous. It was nothing more than an exotic clip-joint. There were 'hostesses' sitting at the tables, encouraging customers to drink themselves into insolvency – I wonder if that was their way of going into 'liquidation'? If you wanted a 'short', such as whisky or brandy, you had to buy the bottle – and that would cost you £100! It had already cost you £35 to get in – a fee that bought you admission and a meal – so it could turn out to be rather an expensive evening out.

The Sheka Fah Nous cabaret, you might expect, would be in keeping with the red-light district in which the club was situated – but it wasn't at all. The clients liked to laugh on their nights out and that is why we were engaged to be there. We were glad when we reached the end of our run, though!

We spent a month in Teheran and were followed everywhere by young people aged from eight to their early twenties. They were fans who flocked to see my films at the local cinemas where they were being shown regularly. They used to follow us down the road shouting, "Mr Norman! Hello Mr Norman!"

In Rhodesia, as it was then, I met Prime Minister Ian Smith, who led the rebellion and declared UDI from Britain. He did not consult me on all this, of course, but he struck me as being a man who genuinely could have done without all the fuss and bother. He loved England and appeared not to want to fall out. Circumstance often seems to lead people to do things that they really don't want to do. Sad old life sometimes, isn't it? Among my souvenirs I still have Ian Smith's autograph. He signed it, 'To Norman from Smudger Smith'.

My films have proved popular in the Far East and I have

travelled the Orient – No! Not Leyton Orient! Everyone there is very polite and have this strange habit of not applauding a single thing until you have completed your act. You know that they are enjoying what you do because you can hear them laughing but, when you finish, there is an eerie moment before they break into very loud applause. Perhaps these days they are a little different since there has been so much Western influence on their culture – but it was a strange experience when I was last there!

In 1972 we were in South Africa. *The Norman Wisdom Show* included Tony Fayne, comic Joe Church, Eddie Calvert with his golden trumpet, and that lovely singer Julie Rogers. In Johannesburg, I thought that they were expecting trouble because there were, what I thought, rather a lot of fire extinguishers in the wings. On closer inspection the 'fire extinguishers' turned out to be oxygen cylinders. The high altitude meant that the dancers had breathing difficulties and so the cylinders were kept there permanently to help them stay alive!

We played in most of the cities of South Africa. It is a very beautiful country and, hopefully, the future will mean that it can be enjoyed by all its inhabitants as well as its visitors.

Australia is another great country. I have been there seven times and have enjoyed each trip. The popular image of the Aussie is one of rolled-up shirt-sleeves, a can of lager in one hand and some sheep-shears, or a surf-board, in the other. I have met a few like that but the vast majority are a fun-loving people who have no problem with us foreigners and who like to do a fair day's work for a fair day's pay!

My first trip to Australia was in 1973. I didn't know what to expect. It was certainly a hot place where we opened the tour, at the South Sydney Junior League Club – but I was worried that the reception would be a lot cooler than the weather. I need not have worried. It was another of those occasions when my films had already paved the way. From the moment that I walked on stage on the opening night I was given the sort of welcome that makes you really know that you are among friends.

Tony Fayne went deaf on that tour. It was at a small town named Goolamgatta, which is in the general direction of the Great Barrier Reef. The local doctor, who was probably also the local vet, barber and coalman, tried to cure the problem but it was to no avail and we had to perform with Tony lip-reading. Having worked the routine so often, we got through it without mishap and later on his hearing returned. I don't know what the problem was but I can only assume that he thought it was his turn to buy a round!

Like most people, I have good and bad memories of my travels – but mostly they are good. I am still asked to go globe-trotting but there are only so many months in a year.

Sometimes I accept an engagement on a cruise to the Caribbean. I enjoy these because I perform once or twice on the way out, we enjoy the islands while we are there, and then do one or two performances on the way back. Most of the time we are free to enjoy all the facilities of the ship and to muck in with everyone else – which means a bit of time in the swimming pool, some deck games, the gym, and a bit of jogging around the deck – on top of all that, I get paid! Some artistes don't like doing cruises because, they say, they get bored. I promise you… I don't!

One of my unlikeliest journeys in recent years has to be my trip to Albania in January 1995. I kept getting invitations from that country for a long time before I finally agreed to go. I have to say that I am very glad that I finally made it. Once again, my films had proved to be very, very popular in Albania – and they loved the character of Norman Pitkin or, as they call him, Pitkini. I had been asked so many times to visit the place that I finally decided that it was only fair to go. So, one day I found myself packing my case for a trip into the unknown. Albania – here we come!

One of the factors that finally convinced me to make the Albanian trip was that it was so obviously a country in need of help. They are a happy people but their past has meant that they have been pushed down and become one of Europe's urchins. As you already know, I really can relate to that and I hoped that my going to Albania might help to draw attention to a nice country that could really do with a helping hand.

Johnny Mans came on the trip with me, along with pianist Jimmy Noon and my old Army pal Pat Dickinson. We did not know what to expect when we flew in to Tirana Airport and I was amazed that among the first people to greet us was a group of armed guards. "What's going on here?" I thought. It looked as if we were about to be arrested.

When we stepped out of the clearance area, I could see why we had these soldiers around us. They were a guard of honour. The place was in uproar. Until that moment I thought that they had just liked my films and were happy for me to visit their country. But it was much more than that! I discovered that I was their favourite film star and I was getting the same reception as the Beatles used to get in Britain and America in the 1960s.

I have never been mobbed like that before. There were masses of people, cheering, clapping, crying, shouting welcome messages, jumping up and down. I could hardly believe what I was experiencing and it made me feel very, very humble. The love that was coming from these people touched me deeply and I wanted to hug every one of them.

I was to be interviewed by television as soon as I arrived and the presenter was doing his best when suddenly he stopped and asked me for my autograph. When I first appeared from the plane I wore my Gump suit – and nearly had it swiped in the mêlée.

I tripped over my feet a few times, fell down some stairs and pretended to run away – and they loved it. And I instantly loved them! They all called me Mr Pitkini but that was okay – I was enjoying myself and had found an army of new mates. One young lady even described me as 'sexy'. Can you imagine that? I looked around for an interpreter in case the word meant something else in Albanian!

We stayed in what was the former dictator's palace, which

was a little ironic really since it was mostly because of him that I had found such unexpected adulation in this corner of the world.

The dictator was Enver Hoxha and he had ruled the communist regime for forty-five years. He was a bit paranoid about Western influences and made it an imprisonable offence for anyone to turn their television aerials toward Italy, across the Adriatic. Albanians could only watch what Hoxha said they could watch. Incredibly, among his favourites were my films, which he considered to be innocent of immorality or subversive political messages. And that's how Pitkini became a household name in Albania.

The trip was put together by a number of British charities and, during my four days in Albania, I visited a number of hospitals, children's homes and other similar welfare projects. It was quite an eye-opener!

On my first day I went to what is known as No 1 Hospital Tirana, a decaying but huge estate, which would probably be condemned in this country. I dread to think how it would rate on a scale of hygiene. British patients would get a real culture shock if they were sent there – everything is so archaic, and looks it! The doctors smoke as they are doing their rounds and the whole place makes our National Health Service seem more like Harley Street.

In the eye unit I met Elton Kola, then aged fourteen, whose right eye had been damaged by a stone. Young Elton was very cheerful, though, and we soon became good pals, as indeed I did with everyone at the hospital.

Our next stop was Child Hope, a project for the 'street children', kids who are going through similar problems to the ones I faced when I was a boy. It seems to be a growing world problem, homeless children with no prospects. The Child Hope project has been set up in Albania to, at least, try to do something about it there.

Also on my trip to Albania, I unveiled a plaque for the Pitkini Centre, another welfare centre sponsored by various charities.

I received a nice tribute from Teodor Loco, Albania's Minister of Culture, Youth and Sport. It was at a dinner held in my honour at the former palace. He said, "His art is above all politics. Totalitarianism is very down, very dark. The humour that came from him was like a light, like a joy for us. It is well known that people need humour in their times of difficulty. For twenty-five years he has been giving us that humour."

I hope so, I really hope so!

It wasn't all dinners and hospitals on that trip. I had a lot of fun as well. I visited some interesting museums and other places that hopefully one day will encourage tourism in Albania and help their finances. I played with the kids in an orphanage and even had a go on the slide in their playground. Any excuse to enjoy myself!

At the Academy of Fine Art I once again had a tremendous reception and was very touched by the love that I received. Like most of Albania, the building was rather run down and even had bats living in the large room which was used for performances.

There was nothing run-down about the performance that was put on by the students of that academy, though! They covered everything from opera to comedy. At the end of their wonderful show I went on stage. I didn't have a clue as to what I was going to do, but I couldn't just go on and say thank you – so I ad-libbed a bit!

I went on and faced the back-drop for a moment, as if I was bewildered, then I turned round and faked shock and fear at seeing the audience. Slowly, I gained confidence, tripped and hit my head on the microphone. Then I made my little speech of thanks and appreciation – not just for that night, but for my entire trip to Albania. I gave Jimmy Noon a nod and he sat down at the piano. Then I announced that I would like to sing a little song for them.

I fooled around for a moment and then we launched into the only song I could have sung on such an occasion – *Don't Laugh At Me...*

By the time that I had finished there were few eyes that did not have tears in them – and mine were as moist as anybody's!

I was sorry to leave Albania. The Albanians are lovely people and I sincerely hope that they get the support that they deserve and are able to bring up the standard of welfare in their country that they are trying so hard to do. Thanks Albania!... Here's to the next time!

That was not the last of my unusual trips abroad. In Chernobyl there is a Norman Wisdom Centre and I desperately wanted to visit it. Since the notorious Chernobyl disaster in 1986 the area has been a wasteland – but an inhabited wasteland! Nobody had ever heard of Chernobyl before that terrible nuclear disaster – but they have now! In general conversation, the name of the place is spoken of almost with contempt, but it is not the fault of the local residents that the disaster took place. They, however, have borne the brunt of the problem and its after effects.

I am patron of International Aid Services which is based on the Isle of Man. It is the charity behind the Norman Wisdom Children's Hospice in the little town of Mayak, near Odessa. It is believed to be the world's largest children's hospice and has 200 beds. International Aid regularly sends convoys to help both the hospice and three other hospitals in the region. I thought that it was high time that I took a look. I have been very impressed with the work of International Aid Services, which has been credited with saving the lives of more than 150 people in the area. The charity has never had much more than £22,000 in the bank, but has still managed to do a tremendous amount of work.

Volunteers give up their annual holidays to go and take part in construction and repair work. Businessmen donate blankets, food and equipment. It is an amazing success story. If International Aid Services has been able to provide vital support for three hospitals, save many lives and build the world's biggest children's hospice, with just £22,000 in the bank, just imagine what it could do if it had a million. We could work miracles with that sort of money!

I wanted to do my bit, so in May 1995, I joined a team of eighty people aboard three trucks and two coaches for the long haul to Chernobyl. I knew that it was going to be a rough journey, but I have lived rough before and this was for a really good cause.

They knew that I was coming and a lot of the kids were excited because, just as in Albania, they had often seen 'Mr Pitkin' on television. But I doubt if even they were as excited as I was!

The journey began at Brinscall, near Chorley in Lancashire, and we hit the road to Felixstowe to pick up the ferry. For me it was a bit like being back in the Army, travelling in convoy with your fellow squaddies. We passed through Germany and then Poland. I told you that it was going to be rough – we didn't use hotels or guest-houses, we slept in the trucks. Whatever money is spent on these missions is channelled directly into the job in hand – there is no way that it can become a tourist trip!

Eventually we reached Chernobyl – and what a place it turned out to be. It must once have been very beautiful but now there is an atmosphere of desolation. There are still people living there but most of them are elderly. I asked one lady why it was that she was still living in this 'ghost area'.

"Where would I go? What would I do? I have never been anywhere else in my entire life and I am much too old to start now! I just have to stay here and do my best to keep myself alive until it is no longer necessary!"

There were a number of elderly people with the same point of view. They decided to live out their days in a place that has already died ahead of them. Our convoy was there to bring them some measure of relief and I felt very privileged to be a part of it.

At Mayak I met the children! They laughed, they chattered and they bravely battled on against all their various illnesses and infirmities. They also smiled away their emotional pains. I admired them greatly and we managed to have some fun and games together.

It had taken six days to travel to the hospice and we stayed there for a further three, unloading supplies and continuing construction and repair work. Some of those who journey out remain there until the next convoy. Once unloaded we had the return journey ahead, once again sleeping rough, getting investigated at the borders and facing up to all sorts of experiences that such an operation brings before you.

I respected those people who do this kind of work even before I journeyed with them but, having been there and seen them in action, I cannot really express the depth of my admiration for them. Thank goodness that there are still such people who are prepared to put themselves out in their efforts to help others.

I am not sure where my next travels will be taking me. I am due in Spain this autumn of 1996 for Henry Cooper's Charity Golf Classic and, every day, there are airmail letters from all parts of the world asking me to pay them a visit.

Who knows? My next stop might be China – but I think I'll wait until after Hong Kong has been handed back – I like my visits to be sweet rather than sour!

At Home

THEY say that home is where the heart is! If that's the case then I must have lots of homes all over the world. I live on the Isle of Man simply because I fell in love with the place when I came here to do a show in Douglas.

As you know, Freda and I lived in a caravan for some years because it was much easier to take our home with us than to keep finding places to stay for the various summer, autumn, panto and spring seasons. When you are in London for a couple of months, and then in Blackpool, followed by Scarborough, followed by a theatre tour, it is a nightmare – especially for your wife – if you have to keep on packing and unpacking your belongings and living in places that you can never really call home because you never stay there long enough.

Finding sites for a caravan, which is your very own established home on wheels, is much easier. When we were between engagements, or working in the London area, we had a regular site at Barnet – and we lived in that caravan, quite happily and comfortably, until 1954 when we thought it was probably time that we bought a house. In truth, we were both a little reluctant to leave our caravan which we had grown to love – but it was time to move on.

Only a couple of miles from our caravan site we found a nice bungalow in Arkley – Galley Lane to be precise. I like Spanish-style buildings and always have done. Don't ask me why, it's just one of those things. This bungalow had just such a hacienda-style about it and I took to it straight away. It had a lovely garden with a goldfish pond, a Japanese plum tree, an apple tree, lawns and a nice conservatory that overlooked the whole thing.

We both liked the house and agreed a price there and then. Within a few weeks we had moved in and had to buy a lot of furniture because there is not much call for it in a caravan and we were virtually starting from scratch. It can be quite good fun buying furniture together and we were like a couple of newly-weds setting up our first home.

Our son, Nicholas, had been born on 18 March 1953, and that was one of the reasons why we had decided to move out of the caravan. I take my hat off to circus and fairground people who successfully raise their families in caravans while they are travelling from place to place every few days. It can't be easy. On 21 December 1954, we welcomed another new arrival – our daughter, Jacqueline, and I could not have been happier.

In 1957 we decided that we had, perhaps, outgrown our bungalow and we heard of an historic house in Sussex. I had taken a flat in Kensington because of the need to get to Pinewood early each morning and I kept the flat on even though it had become more of an office than a dwelling.

The house in Sussex was a 15th-century farmhouse where Henry VIII had installed Anne of Cleves for a while. It was an amazing place. You could feel the history impregnated into the walls and when you looked out of the window you wondered about the others who, throughout the centuries, had stood on the same spot.

The house stood – and still stands – in West Chiltington, in its own grounds of twelve acres. The village itself is quite historic and, in its centre, there can still be seen the old stocks. I bet I would have ended up in them if I had been alive all those years ago!

Although I am a 'townie' by origin, I have always loved the countryside and Sussex was a beautiful county in which I found that I could relax. The local people got used to having me around and treated me like one of their own. If I slipped into a country pub for a quiet evening with friends, I was left alone to enjoy myself. It was a lovely place with lovely people.

The property was also a great place for the children. Nick became a pupil at Charterhouse and Jackie eventually went to the Royal Naval College for Ladies at Petworth. At home they had plenty of space to develop and, of course, Jacqui had her own pony – something which I could hardly refuse as we had stables and since I had also enjoyed my riding experiences in the Army. I could hardly deny her the same pleasure. Nick followed in my sporting footsteps and later played cricket at county level for Sussex. Today he owns a sports shop in Haywards Heath and, naturally, I am a frequent visitor. Jacqui became an air hostess for a time but her interest in art led her to working in a dealers in Mayfair. She is still in that same field.

I did not put pressure on my children to follow in my footsteps. If they had decided to come into showbusiness then I would have encouraged them – but no more than I have for the paths that they have chosen. I am very proud of them both and their families – yes, I'm a grandad, and when we're all together I'm as daft as I was when I was a kid. When you get your own bike busted when you are a kid, you can't wait to buy one for your own kids and your grandchildren so that you can make up for the times when you didn't get a chance to have a go on your own bike! I'll leave that to your imagination! I still think that train sets, bikes, scooters and lollies are among life's special treasures. Pass the Dolly Mixtures, please!

America was good to me as far as my career was concerned but, as I told you earlier in the book, it probably cost me my marriage. I thought that everything was fine between Freda and me. We had come through some pretty uncertain times together and we were now quite comfortable. I think it was the time I spent on *Walking Happy* that caused the problem. I was involved with that show for twenty-one months. It was decided that Freda would stay in England with the children – but we still saw each other during breaks and spoke frequently on the phone. But it wasn't enough and Freda found consolation with someone else, probably someone tall, dark and handsome – the complete opposite of me.

I realised too late that I had made the mistake of allowing my work to rule my life. I learned a hard lesson from that. You have to get your priorities right. It has been said to me that if I had continued in America they would have taken me to the same status as people like Jack Lemmon and Walter Matthau or Robin Williams. It has also been suggested that my walking away from Hollywood made room for Peter Sellers to move in. I don't know! It's all history now anyway!

In February 1969, the divorce judge awarded me a decree nisi and, at the same time, decided that the children were old enough to decide which of us they wanted to live with. I was very moved when they chose me! Although we were divorced, Freda and I did not become enemies. She saw the children regularly and we kept in touch, sometimes getting together for a family meal. In short, we remained friends until she sadly died just a couple of years ago.

We continued to live at West Chiltington and I employed a 'nanny', who became known to us all as 'Magic'. She was a widow and the mother of a former secretary of mine, and she kept house for us. She came on a four-week trial and was still with us six years later. Madge Perodeau was her name, and she was ideal for us – especially her cooking!

Another misadventure in the late 1960s was my battle with the taxman. I was not the first, and certainly not the last, to fall foul of the dreaded Inland Revenue. I am not, and never have been, a tax dodger! I am a very loyal and patriotic subject of both Her Majesty, and Her Majesty's Government – whoever happens to be in power.

The trouble was that for every pound I earned I had to pay eighteen shillings and sixpence in tax. By today's finances that would mean that I would have seven and a half pence to myself from every pound earned. My financial advisors looked at every legal way of saving me some money and came up with a scheme in which I could, perfectly legitimately, buy silver bullion as an investment, without having to pay tax on the profit I made from the sale of it later.

The estimated profit was £20,000 – but the actual profit realised was £50,000. I was stunned and the Inland Revenue were not too happy. They sent me another huge tax bill, which we immediately contested. In March 1968 we faced each other in court and the judge found in my favour – even awarding me costs. But the taxmen were not to be beaten and eight months later we were back at the Court of Appeal. It didn't appeal to me very much but the Inland Revenue found it very appealing and persuaded the three appeal judges that I should pay tax on my profits. This time I lost, but I felt so aggrieved that I wanted to take the matter to the House of Lords. The judges refused me leave to do that – and so I was snookered!

There were quite a few newspaper columns about it, and some of them seemed to suggest that I had been trying to avoid paying income tax, which was definitely not the case! My advisors were simply taking advantage of the rules which had been set up by the Inland Revenue in the first place.

There was some revenge later because Ken Bowers, my pal and financial advisor, swore that he would get even for, what he felt was, my getting 'stitched up' by the Inland Revenue. He established me as a metal trader and somehow that helped me with investments which the taxman had no chance of touching – all perfectly legal!

To be honest, I didn't understand any part of it! I knew that, as an entertainer, I, and others like me, were being heavily penalised for getting paid to help more people enjoy themselves. I left all my financial affairs in the capable hands of my advisors with the sole provision and assurance that nothing illegal would take place. To this day I believe that nothing illegal ever did take place!

Because I now live on the Isle of Man, some people assume that I moved here in a huff to avoid paying tax in Britain. That is far from the truth – and I do, in fact, pay tax to the British Government – because I also have an apartment in Epsom and most of my money is earned in Britain! As a kid, I was driven to dishonesty to avoid starvation but since then, I have never knowingly crossed the border into illegality for any reason!

My move to the Isle of Man in 1980 was more of an accident than anything else. I was surprised to find that I had never been here before 1977. I thought that I had been just about everywhere, but when a three-month summer season at the Gaiety Theatre, Douglas, was offered to me, I suddenly realised that this island of TT racing, Manx cats and three legs was completely strange to me – even though it was on the doorstep of Britain.

I came to the Isle of Man, had a wonderful summer season, and explored the island. What a beautiful place! I fell in love with it, and the more I thought about it the more I realised that I would be very happy living there. It was like England, thirty years earlier. Everyone was friendly. The only crime wave was when a policeman waved at you from across the street! The landscape was breathtaking and, to me, I had found my paradise!

I made up my mind that I would make the move. The family were old enough to do their own thing and there would be a roof over their heads with me any time they wanted it. I found a suitable plot in the fairly remote area of Kirk Andreas on the North-West coast and then I rented a house in Bride, while I sorted out the various planning permissions for the new home which I had designed myself.

It took some time, and then there was a further eighteen months for the house to be built. So it was, finally, not until 1984 that I was able to have a house-warming – but it was well worth the wait! It would be nice to have you all visit, but then, it might make me feel that I was living in a stately home and give me ideas above my station.

I could not resist a touch of the hacienda about the place and, with the use of Manx stone and other types too, the house really looks as if it has been standing for a good many years. The view is across a lovely valley to the distant hills and I often spend a relaxing hour just looking out at, what I find to be, one of the most picturesque scenes that I have ever witnessed.

Just to give you a guided tour of 'Ballalaugh', which is the name of my house, I have the usual bedrooms and bathrooms with space enough for guests without going over the top and making the place feel like a guest-house. I have tried to capture the Spanish style that I love by the interior design as well as by the choice of furniture. There is a nice patio with green and brown tiles, which blend together well to fit in with the colours of the lawns and trees.

I have a study where I catch up with my paper-work, answer letters, read scripts and so on. Above my desk is a framed telegram from the family of the wonderful Sid Field, who was one of my favourite comics. Sid died in 1950 and when I appeared at the Prince of Wales Theatre in April 1952, I was thrilled to be using his old dressing-room from his many days of almost-residency at that great theatre.

About half-an-hour before the opening performance a telegram was delivered to my dressing-room. It read: 'If anyone can take his place, we think it's you. Every success. Sid Field Family.'

It was a marvellous gesture and made me feel elated before I went on stage. I treasured that telegram and that is why it has such a special place above my desk.

My study has oak panelling and all around the room are framed theatre posters and photographs – all of which have special meaning for me. You can go from the study to the summer-house, where I like to have some reading time.

I think that you would probably like the lounge. It is my favourite room and is dominated by my lovely French Erard grand piano. I still write songs and will often sit at my piano to work – but also quite often simply to play and enjoy myself.

Also in the lounge is a display cabinet in which I keep some of my trophies. You can see the British Academy Award and a set of engraved silver spoons, given to me by Paddy Carstairs – one for each film that we made together. There is the Lifetime Achievement Award – given to me by fellow comics, seven Top Comedian Awards, The Golden Flame from Argentina, and miscellaneous other bits of silverware which have given me much pleasure and satisfaction.

Show off, ain't I?

On one wall is a painting of me as Aladdin at the London Palladium. I am kneeling in a spotlight. It is a wonderful piece that was painted in 1956 by Francis Russel Flint. In the painting I am holding the magic lamp and you can also see that in my display cabinet. It is the one presented to me by Bernard Delfont at the end of that record-breaking panto season.

The lounge also has bay windows which I have always liked and made sure were included in my plans. As well as the obvious settees and armchairs, I also have an enormous television set. It probably sounds as if I'm a bit of a layabout, especially when I tell you that I have Barbara, my secretary, minder, nanny, housekeeper, rolling-pin-wielder, head cook and bottle-washer, to keep the place in order, and Rodney, the gardener, who performs wonders in keeping the exterior looking wonderful throughout the year and also provides me with a breathtaking display of colour during the summer months when the flower beds are at their magnificent best.

All right, perhaps I am a layabout when it comes to the domestic side of things – but I do keep myself busy with everything else. I like to walk or jog up to five miles a day – and I try to do that wherever I am. I do my best to keep fit. I exercise every day and I watch my diet. For six days every week I keep active and keep an eye on what I eat. On the seventh day I let my flesh creep and eat whatever I like!

After travelling so much, my taste buds will turn to just about everything. I love what I call a 'curry-up'. I don't mind how hot it is just so long as I don't have to call the fire brigade! Dear old Roy Castle was the best curry eater that I have ever met. He used to love it – and the hotter the better. I remember one Saturday night in Bournemouth in 1970, we arranged to meet at an Indian restaurant after the show. I got there first and bribed the manager, whom I knew, to fix for Roy the curry to end all curries. He didn't need asking twice – he relished the challenge.

Roy turned up and got stuck into the specially prepared curry while I sat back and waited for the explosion. Nothing happened! He finished the lot and thoroughly enjoyed it. Not only was I amazed but so was the restaurant owner who couldn't believe his own eyes and thought that he had failed miserably!

I have been known to create a fair curry myself. That has surprised you hasn't it? The secret is out. For all these years I have pretended that I could never become one of the Roux Brothers, whereas in fact I am a mean man in the kitchen! You just lead me to the kitchen and leave me with a few ingredients and I'll have something on the table in no time at all. Mind you, I do have to specify that the ingredients must include a tin-opener, Heinz soup, a frozen meal from Marks and Spencer, and a microwave!

I love ordinary English cooking – stews, steak and kidney pudding, sausage and mash, roasts, shepherd's pie, egg and chips and, of course, the best meal of the lot – fish and chips! There's a good chip shop near my flat in Epsom and I am a regular customer when I am staying there.

I can eat 'nouveau cuisine' with the best of them – but you can't beat good old fish and chips!

Another of my pastimes is riding my motorbike. I like to go for a spin round the Isle of Man, but not in the TT races – I wouldn't want to show anybody up! I learned to ride a motorbike when I was in the Army and I used to have a bike with me when I was filming at Pinewood. You can get pretty bored when you are having a long break between scenes, so I used to take my bike round the country lanes and open up the throttle.

You didn't have to wear a helmet in those days and the feeling of the wind blowing through your hair was wonderful. Nowadays you have to go out looking like an astronaut! It makes sense really though! Getting a dent in your helmet is better than getting one in your head! I still take to my motorbike quite regularly. I came off it in 1995. There was no harm done, but it might have been a bit more polite if the bloke who was behind the wheel of the car that hit me had actually asked me if I was all right!

When they get around to filming the sequel to *Easy Rider*, I'll be the first in the queue to star in it – but they'll have to call it 'Wheezy Rider'!

I am a car fanatic as I've already said. I always have been! I rarely miss a motor show and when we are travelling I like to visit all the car showrooms. At home I have a Rolls-Royce Silver Spirit. When I first moved to the Isle of Man I still had my Bentley Continental – but I later sold it. I wish that I'd kept it because it was a real beauty and would look a picture in my garage alongside my Rolls. I do not use the Rolls that often, but it is a lovely car to drive and sometimes I'll go for a trip round the island just for the sheer pleasure of driving it.

In addition to my keep-fit programme and driving about, I like to read – but, if it is put-your-feet-up-time, then I get a few sandwiches and spread myself out in front of the giant television in the lounge. I suppose I could have gone to live in the South of France or Spain, but the truth is that on the Isle of Man you can get *Match of the Day* – in English!

My television viewing is chiefly sport – I am still a fanatic. I do watch the soaps a bit but I can never keep track of them too closely because I sometimes go weeks without being in during the evenings. I know I could video the episodes but I'd never have the time to catch up. One soap that really did capture my interest was *Dallas*. I used to enjoy that. I thought that it was well-produced and well-acted with some excellent characters. The incessant rivalry between J.R.Ewing and Cliff Barnes was gripping stuff! I quite enjoyed *Neighbours* for a while but, as the cast became younger and younger, I started to feel like an intruder.

I am a news freak and will watch the news every hour, on the hour. I like to know what is going on in the world. I also like current affairs programmes and will watch *Question Time* just to disagree with everyone. I meet politicians quite often and most of them are decent, down-to-earth people when you meet them privately – but so many have a public face that often hides a much better side to their personality... It's a shame!

I like to watch films on television. I'll give most things a try that fall into the category of family entertainment. I especially like the old musicals and never tire of watching them. When you watch people like Fred Astaire or Gene Kelly, you are seeing sheer genius! It is a pity that they could not go on for ever because there is no one to touch them today!

Having said all this about television, don't think for a moment that I'm an addict because I am not at all! I only put the television on when there is something that I particularly want to watch. If one of my own films is being shown I rarely put it on unless I have a visitor who wants to see it. I have all my films on video so I can see them whenever I want!

My apartment at Epsom is not far from the famous Epsom Downs. It is in a quiet spot, handy for the shops, useful for getting into Central London, but also a nice place to escape to at the end of the day!

I like my homes but especially the one on the Isle of Man. When I fly home and the plane touches down on the island, it really feels that I have arrived home and I begin to relax even before the plane comes to a standstill.

As I have said before, my lifestyle enables me to suffer in comfort!

I like to meet people and on the Isle of Man I have been accepted as a local. In January 1994, I was given the Freedom of the Borough of Douglas – an honour which has only been given to a few people like Winston Churchill, Montgomery and Lord Derby. The, then, Mayor of Douglas, Councillor George Chattal, and his wife Rainer, hosted the event at the Royal Hall, Villa

Marina, at which I was given the Freedom and I felt both honoured and humbled to think that these lovely people had made me one of their own.

I am often asked to take part in holiday programmes for television, talking about the Isle of Man. I never refuse if I can help it. I like the idea of other people enjoying a week or two on this wonderful island.

The Isle of Man stole my heart in 1977 and, if home is where the heart is, then I am certainly living in the right place.

Sporting Wisdom

WHAT in the world is Norman Wisdom doing writing about sport in his autobiography? Well, sport has always been a major part of my life and I could not just ignore that! Also, I always wanted to write a sports column for a newspaper – or appear as one of those panel of experts on television. Nobody would ever ask me so I thought I would do a bit of sports writing here – just to show them what they're missing!

My sports interests go back to being a kid and playing football in the street. That came flooding back to me when I was shooting *On The Beat*. There is a sequence in which a bunch of kids get me to referee their game of soccer in the street. Of course, I end up using the police whistle and that sparks off a whole chain of hilarious events. In between takes I used to kick about with the lads and, I can tell you, that took me back a few years!

As a boy, I followed Arsenal and I still keep an eye on their results even now. I have made appearances at quite a lot of football grounds and even donned Manchester City kit for a bit of fun a few years ago. But one of my most memorable moments was stepping on to the pitch at Highbury and kicking a policeman's helmet from one end to the other while being chased by a bunch of coppers! It was all a pre-arranged stunt, but it was still a lot of fun to score a goal – even if it was a helmet that crossed the goal-line! The crowd loved it!

In the Army I had a wonderful time. I've already told you about my boxing exploits, but we also had a go at everything we could and I spent many happy hours playing football, cricket, running, swimming – you name it and I did it! I played on the wing when I was on the football pitch. I was quite fast and could cross a ball pretty well. Sometimes I would play as an inside-forward – or midfielder as they are called these days.

I wasn't much of a bowler when we played cricket, but I wasn't too bad at the wicket and I was quite nippy in the field. I enjoyed cross-country running and won a few races in my time. I have always believed in maintaining fitness which is why I continue to make the effort now.

Much of my sports interest nowadays is taken up simply by watching. In 1976, when I was living in Sussex, I was invited to join the board of Brighton & Hove Albion Football Club. I was very keen because I always wanted to be involved in the running of a football club. I was there for six years and I really enjoyed it, although I don't know if my presence was of any benefit to the club! We discussed a lot. Our board meetings were really inter-esting if you liked talking about the tea-rooms or whether or not the toilets should be painted during the close season.

I was more interested in the activities of the team, but this seemed to be a taboo subject – mostly because managers seem to jealously guard their control of all playing matters. They always appear to avoid talking about anything to do with the team unless it is to ask for more money with which to buy a player or two.

In fairness, many a director thinks that he knows more about football than the professionals that are employed to do the job – so I do understand the lack of communication from both sides.

You might think that I miss watching top-class football since I moved to the Isle of Man, but that is not the case. I watch local games now and then but I also see some pretty good stuff when I visit my pal, Pat Dickinson. He and I used to play in the same

Army soccer team and have been good mates ever since. He lives in Newcastle so that will give you a good idea of where we go to watch a football match.

In the last few seasons the soccer has been really exciting at St James's Park. I have been to a number of games and I really thought that the championship of the Premiership was on its way to Newcastle in 1996 – but in the end it was not to be! Kevin Keegan and Terry McDermott have done a fantastic job in changing the fortunes of Newcastle since they took over and I'm sure it will not be long before they are holding a major trophy.

It must be said that Sir John Hall has also done a great job in the development of the club – especially that wonderful stadium which has been transformed into a real super soccer arena. Whenever I go to Newcastle I am always overwhelmed by the marvellous Geordie hospitality and I would like to say a public 'Thank you' to everyone at the club for their extremely friendly welcome.

I watch a lot of football on television. I enjoy the live matches on Sky, but life would not be the same without *Match of the Day*. I rarely miss it! I was glued to the television for Euro '96. Germany did well to win it, but the European Championship could have gone to almost any of the sixteen countries taking part, including England. Let's hope for better fortune in the World Cup.

My apologies to anyone who doesn't like football. Let's talk about tennis instead! I've never been much good at playing tennis, but I do enjoy a game. Mostly, I enjoy watching Wimbledon. There is something really special about the atmosphere of the Wimbledon fortnight. You can smell the grass and almost taste the strawberries and cream. I love it and I try to watch as much as I can. What I miss during the day I catch up with at night in the highlights programme.

It is disappointing that, year after year, the singles finals are contested between people from overseas – but one of these days there will be a Briton to cheer on again, I'm sure! After the 1996 Wimbledon it looks like being the up-and-coming Tim Henman.

What about cricket? I'm a member of the Lords Taverners and love to spend a day at a top cricket match. When I was travelling to South Africa with Tony Fayne in 1972, we were on the same plane as the Australian cricket team and it was good to spend some of the journey chatting to them. Cricket is a patient game and very relaxing to watch. It is almost like watching a chess match but with a whole lot more activity!

English cricket seems to have gone through a bad spell in recent years but it seems that things are improving in this season of 1996. Before long the rest of the world will be fearful of us again! Optimistic?... Of course I am!

My chief sporting activity these days, apart from some jogging and cycling, is golf! I love it and, like most golfers, I could spend all day and every day following that little white ball around the course.

I was first introduced to golf when I was at Scarborough in summer season. We used to have a bit of time to ourselves during the day and, often, groups of the cast would organise some activity such as swimming or the odd trip out somewhere. One day it was golf! I hired some clubs and had a go – finding myself surprisingly useless! That was it – a new challenge!

Later, when I was at Pinewood, I used to see a lot of Sean Connery who was filming one of his famous James Bond spectaculars. Sean is a very good golfer and we did quite a few rounds together. He certainly showed me how to improve my game.

Every year the Norman Wisdom Classic is staged at Mottram Hall near Manchester, and a gathering of sports and showbusiness stars turn out to raise money for charities. One of the joys of golf is its friendliness. When you are out on the course the game is between you, the ball, and the course. It doesn't matter how anybody else is scoring. Other players will give you tips as you compete against them. Can you imagine that happening in any other sport?

There is a great love of golf among showbusiness people with several showbiz teams. Hardly a day goes by without some charity or other being boosted by the presence of one or two celebrities at a tournament somewhere. Jimmy Tarbuck is probably the top showbiz golfer. He is mad keen on the game and spends as much time as possible on the course. He also has some special golf days for charity.

Another very good golfer is Alan Randall. He is a regular tournament winner along with Pete Langford of the Barron Knights. There are also some good golfers from the sports world, among them former footballers Ray Clemence, Kenny Dalglish, Ian St John and Billy Bremner. From today's footballers there are Niall Quinn, Gary McAllister – who was a Scottish schoolboy golf international – Gary Speed and countless others. Footballers take to golf very well, but then, so do cricketers – and Wasim Akram, of Lancashire and Pakistan, took up the game in 1995 and is said to be pretty hot stuff on the course.

One of the top manufacturers of golf clubs is Karsten Solheim – an American gentleman who revolutionised putters. In Britain, his company, Karsten (UK) Ltd, is based in the unlikely setting of Gainsborough in Lincolnshire. I went along there to see how they make their famous Ping golf clubs.

I was amazed. It was like watching a suit being made. When I first arrived they took me into an indoor driving area and took a few notes. Then they showed me around some of the vast factory, whisked me off to lunch at the nearby Gainsborough Golf Club – which is owned by the company. Then I saw the rest of the factory and, before I left, they presented me with a superb set of made-to-measure clubs. I was completely flabbergasted because I had not expected anything like that. I was just interested to see how it was done and I was very touched by their wonderful gift. Thank you Roy Freeman and Glen Batkin.

I am a member of two golf clubs on the Isle of Man. My handicap is about 18 and I always carry two putters – one to try to get the ball in the hole and the other to fling when I miss! Golfers will know exactly what I mean.

Boxing is another big love of mine. We have already talked

about my Army days in the ring and I sometimes wonder how it would have turned out if I had pursued a boxing career instead of one in showbusiness. Can you imagine the MC?

"Ladies and Gentlemen! Introducing in the blue corner – the heavyweight champion of the world!... Norman Wisdom!"

Oh well, I can dream can't I? Anyway, at least I know how to fall!

Some people say that sportsmen are too highly paid these days – but you have to move with the times a little! Professional sports people attract very large crowds in stadiums and arenas. It is their career, their chosen life, a way of earning from what they do best. A skilled tradesman – a bricklayer for instance – can use his talent for forty years or more – two or three times as long as a sportsman. So, providing that the sportsman is giving of his or her best, I think they do deserve good money while they're able to earn it. That's just my opinion for what it's worth!

There are other recreations in addition to sport and, if you want to keep fit, how about a spot of dancing? There are no longer the dancers around as there used to be a few years back. Dancing is pretty energetic, especially if you get into tap dancing – and if you are young enough you could even carve a career out of it.

I mentioned earlier about the lack of dancers. You don't see the perfection of people like Fred Astaire or Gene Kelly any more, or the wonderful sequences that can be seen in films like *Seven Brides For Seven Brothers*, *Singin' In The Rain* and other great musicals.

Having said that, when you see a show like *Riverdance* it gives you renewed hope for the future. If you haven't seen it live, it really is worth the effort of going. Michael Flatley, who was one of the originators of the show, now has his own touring company. Michael is excellent, how I wish there were a few more like him. *Riverdance* has breathed new life into dancing and long may it be successful.

As you will have gathered by now, I like life to be fun and that is why I am so keen on sport and physical recreation. They won't let me play football any more, but as long as I can still run and cycle I am happy to enjoy that.

Not too long ago, I put on my ice-skates again. It was at the special invitation of the Russian Ice-Stars, who were performing *The Phantom Of The Opera* on ice at the Labbatt's Apollo in Hammersmith. I put the skates on and had a go to see if I could still do it. I couldn't really refuse because it turned out that most of the ice company were fans of my films.

I was a bit scared because I thought I might slip and damage something that mattered but if I looked as if I might fall, a couple of the girl-skaters held me up. I've never known myself to be so likely to fall before!

I suppose that, at eighty-one, I should be a little less reckless but, as I always say, – you're only young once!

Straightmen
And
Funnymen

SINCE accidentally starting to work with David Nixon all those years ago, I have long appreciated the benefit of appearing with a straight man. I started as a solo artiste and I am still a solo artiste. I have never wanted to be a part of a double act like Morecambe and Wise, Cannon and Ball, Little and Large, or any of the other great comedy duos. Nevertheless, some of my work seems to be at its best when there is a foil – someone to bounce off with both words and actions.

Eddie Leslie was my first straight man and we became good pals, as indeed I did with my other straight men. You may recall that Eddie and I first met in panto and we hit it off straight away. Eddie was a terrific clown in his own right, a larger than life character who was as funny, if not funnier, behind the scenes as he was in performance. I can well remember him once walking through a group of dignitaries wearing just a top hat, a jock strap, socks and swinging a cane. He didn't quite intend it that way. We had shut him out of his dressing-room so he decided to brazen it out anyway – and he got away with it!

On another occasion in panto at Wolverhampton he rendered me helpless with laughter simply by putting his finger through a hole in a bucket. I was crying with laughter and had to leave the stage for a while. The audience never realised that it was not a part of the show – but the director did and he gave us both a good ticking off.

That was Eddie Leslie, a very funny man and a very good friend. As funny as he was, Eddie could play it as straight as anyone when it was needed!

When you do an act like mine, a good straight man is vital. We must be as one with our timing. One misplaced quip can ruin an entire sequence. He must never crack up and find me funny but must always remain aloof, arrogant, intolerant and, above-all, he must keep a straight face. He must also be an artiste in his own right and be able to fill in if there is a problem.

Nicholas Parsons used to be straight man for Arthur Haynes and he did a very good job of it. One night, at the London Palladium, Arthur was taken ill and could not appear. Nicholas Parsons, at very short notice, went on and filled in on his own.

Eddie Leslie was like that. He appeared in many of my films, became heavily involved in scripting and was totally professional in everything that he did. I gave him a hard time when he was trying to keep a straight face but he rarely cracked.

Jerry Desmonde was the same. He was already in the business when I was just a kid, having started in 1919 at the age of eleven. He had teamed up with his brother, Jack, for a song and dance routine, and later became straight man to cockney comic, Gus Elton, and then Scotsman, Dave Willis. In the 1930s he also teamed up with his wife but his biggest break probably came when he teamed up with the wonderful Sid Field in the West End. They appeared together on stage from 1943 to 1946 and then made two films together, *London Town* in 1946, and *The Cardboard Cavalier* in 1947.

By the time Jerry and I got together he was one of the most experienced straight men in the business, having also worked with such stars as Arthur Askey, Nat Jackley and Bob Hope. Anyway, we got together and made six films as well as working together in many stage and television shows. He was a lovely man who also had a great sense of humour. It was tragic when he committed suicide in 1967 and it was a mystery too – he appeared to have such a lot going for him.

In addition to his work with me, Jerry was popular with television viewers who enjoyed his appearances on the ever-popular *What's My Line?* and his hosting of *The 64,000 Dollar Question*. He would always see the funny side of things – which is a sad affliction for a straight man. Jerry had this tremendous ability to keep his face straight even when his eyes were filling with tears of laughter. I often watched his hands grinding into each other in an effort to keep himself under control. As soon as the director shouted "Cut!" Jerry would explode with mirth. He was a great pro!

My straight men need to be a fair bit taller than me and Tony Fayne filled that particular requirement quite nicely. More than six feet tall, he has the look and build of a Grenadier Guardsman, and he towers over me when we are on stage together. Tony began as an impressionist in 1940, making his debut at the Bristol Empire. He worked with David Evans and they had an unusual act which included their own comedy songs and sporting impersonations.

They became a very popular act and played the Palladium in 1951 as a support to Judy Garland. We were on our first show together in 1954. When his partner was taken ill, Tony continued alone from 1959 and made a number of comedy records. He also became a partner of Arthur Haynes for three years.

It was Billy Marsh who suggested that Tony and I might work together, since Billy was his agent too. We launched the idea in 1968 and we are still getting on after nearly thirty years. We have been all over the world together as well as touring throughout Britain. We are both golfers and are very keen on cricket, so we both have a lot of other things in common, as well as being tall, dark and handsome – well, one of us is!

In my films, David Lodge has often been a straight man. He has the same problem as did Jerry Desmonde – a fantastic sense of humour. It was not unusual for him to struggle to complete a scene after something amusing had happened between us. The more he tried to put it out of his mind the funnier it became to him.

David is not only a very fine actor with a great range of experience but he is also a very clever writer. An immensely talented man who has worked – and more than held his own – with the cream of the film industry.

Edward Chapman was, of course, Mr Grimsdale. He was, in essence, a straight man, but tended more to get into trouble with me rather than against me. Edward, again, was a very experienced actor with a sense of fun. He was great to work with and it was a sad loss when he died.

I have had some wonderful straight men who have all turned out to be good mates as well. Who is, or was, my favourite? I can't answer that one! They all had something different to offer. The idea of a straight man is always, basically, the same – but the portrayal is always different. In my book, Eddie Leslie, Jerry Desmonde, Tony Fayne, David Lodge and Edward Chapman, all have star rating!

Another question that I'm often asked is which comics make me laugh. We've had a look at some of the great straight men, so now let's take a look at some of the funny men.

In 1968 we had a very clever, very funny comic on the support bill. After he had worked he used to dash to his dressing-room to get changed, and then he would stand in the wings night after night to watch my act. He became a star – Freddie Starr! Some people say that he based his act around impersonating me, but I can't agree with that. He certainly does do one of the best Norman Wisdom impersonations that I've ever seen, but then again – if he does it straight – he also does a fantastic Elvis impersonation!

In recent years he has gained a bit of a reputation as a tear-away but, when he was a support act on our shows, he was not at all like that. He was a nice young guy with an abundance of talent. I was not at all surprised that he became such a big name. I'm a little disappointed that he has turned to doing 'adult' shows – but that's none of my business.

Going back in time, I like the old Ealing Comedy films and all that kind of innocent fun. I love the Will Hay films. He was a clever man. Not only was he very funny and his films highly successful, but he was quite a leading light in the field of astronomy. Will Hay's films were funny the first time round but they became funnier as you watched them again and again. There are so many subtle lines and expressions that you cannot possibly take them all in at once!

Charlie Chaplin films were, and are, a big favourite of mine of course. That's why I was so keen to meet him when we were in Hollywood. He made me laugh when I first saw his films and he still makes me laugh even now. He was a wonderful clown. Laurel and Hardy had the same appeal. They could take the simplest situation and turn it into an hilarious romp just by adding a little exaggerated mime, a well-timed glance and then, when sound movies came in, some wonderful lines. They don't make them like Chaplin or Laurel and Hardy any more!

Talking of older comedy stars, I did love Sid Field and Will Fyffe. They both had such tremendous comedy talent that they could render an audience totally helpless with laughter. Nat Jackley was another who was a master of his craft. His eccentric walks have been copied by many but bettered by none! I'm not just looking at these comedy stars as artistes. Quite simply, they were funny!

I do not like the move away from fun as a basis for entertainment. There are some artistes now who peddle filth under the guise of showbusiness. There are many incidents in the history of showbusiness where it has been bawdy or risque – but never out-and-out filthy. They call it 'alternative' humour. Well, the only alternative to being funny is not being funny! They call it 'adult'

– in fact it is childish! Hearing someone using foul language in front of lots of other people is the sort of thing that got a giggle in the classroom. Most people grow out of that by the time they have reached their late teens. It seems that it is so much easier to embarrass people into laughing by using that sort of puerile rubbish than it is to sit down and work out something that is genuinely funny. Nowadays we are forced to endure all this rubbish or be classed as boring old so and so's. I prefer being the latter!

Arthur Askey didn't use foul language and he was a brilliantly funny man. He was also one of my favourites, 'Big-Hearted Arthur', they called him and he certainly was. Tommy Cooper didn't have to resort to barrack-room lingo either. What a funny man he was. He only had to appear on stage for the audience to be in stitches. He had a marvellous act which was hardly ever the same two nights running. He really did seem to make it up as he went along. Both Tommy and Arthur were lovely men and they both made me laugh.

Joyce Grenfell was a clever lady, wasn't she? Joyce had a marvellous way of painting a picture out of everyday things. The children's television programme *Blue Peter* has a reputation for teaching kids how to make wonderful and useful things out of old washing-up liquid bottles, toilet-rolls and dead matches. Joyce could do that with words. From nothing she could plant in your mind a classroom full of kids doing all the things that children do – and in the embarrassing way that they seem to do it. She was very funny and a great entertainer too!

Another great talent was Tony Hancock. I was a big fan of *Hancock's Half Hour* on the radio – although I never felt that it made the transfer to television very successfully. Some will say that Tony Hancock was lucky to have had such a good script and a great support cast, but it wasn't only that. Tony was a very talented and funny man with a great delivery. It was no accident that he was the star of that extremely funny radio show!

Eric Morecambe and Ernie Wise formed what was undoubtedly the funniest comedy double act that Britain has produced in recent decades. They worked brilliantly together and I'm sure they would still have been going strong had it not been for the tragic and untimely death of Eric. I loved their stage act and, of course, their marvellous television shows – especially those plays what Ernie wrote!

There is a comedy duo who tour with me regularly. They are the Simmons Brothers, and they are two very funny guys who never fail to have their audience in raptures of laughter. As well as having their own great act with lots of visual humour as well as patter, Keith and Alan write a lot of material for others – including complete pantomimes!

I do enjoy visual humour which is why I laugh at people like Bernie Clifton and Norman Collier. There is a bit of the maniac in all of us and when it is allowed out – it can be hilarious.

To me, humour has to be plausible. As an example, the opening scene of *The Early Bird* is a situation that could happen. It is first thing in the morning. The alarm has stirred Norman into action, although he is not really awake. What follows is twelve minutes without a word of dialogue and, as everyone will have noticed, I keep falling down the stairs. But everything is plausible.

It's in the morning and I'm bleary-eyed and the cord of my dressing-gown gets caught in the door. I give it a tug and as it gives way I hurtle down the stairs. I try to stop myself by grabbing at anything – but the only thing that my hand grabs is a shred of wallpaper which then rips down the wall from the top of the stairs to the bottom.

Later I go down the stairs again, holding a full cup and saucer for Mr Grimsdale. Since it is for my boss I don't want to spill it – and I don't, despite hurtling down the stairs again. It might be slightly over the top but it is plausible – and that is what makes it funny!

In *A Stitch In Time*, I had to masquerade as a nurse to fool Jerry Desmonde, one of the villains of the piece. Make-up did a brilliant job but I'm no Danny La Rue. By exaggerated movements I made sure that it was never lost on the audience that I was Norm dressed up – even if Jerry was fooled for a time. The audience were in on the prank.

One of the best television comedies in recent decades has to be *Fawlty Towers*. The work between John Cleese and Andrew Sachs was simply wonderful. However manic their situations became, they were never impossible and, as such, they were a riot. I still have a good laugh at the videos.

Of the young comics, Joe Pasquale has developed a style all his own, and the audience obviously like him. He makes me laugh too.

I also laugh at Eric Sykes. Over the years he has proved him-self to be a comic genius. His scripting, his visual ideas and his ability to put them into practice are nothing short of marvellous. Just watch repeats of the old programmes that he made with Hattie Jacques. They are still very, very funny!

Another word or two about comedy – Comic Heritage is an organisation with which I am proud to be involved. Comic Herit-age makes sure that Britain's comedy stars are never forgotten. The organisation has its own magazine and annual awards and it also installs plaques in suitable places, such as the birthplaces of various big names of comedy. Comic Heritage also raises a few bob for charity and that can't be a bad thing. If you can have a laugh while you are giving someone else a helping hand, then life seems a whole lot better.

I could go on about comics old and new – The Crazy Gang to name but a few, but where do you draw the line?

Pound for pound I prefer older comedy to today's comedy. Perhaps it is my age but, apart from the bad language, I find it difficult to laugh when people shout their jokes at me – or pull faces for no apparent reason.

There is a young man called Lee Evans who is proving to be very popular. I have often been asked what I think of him as many people say that he is just like me. To be perfectly honest I have never yet seen him so I can't really make any comment, but if you have the ability to make people laugh without having to resort to the things I have mentioned earlier – then I wish you all the best mate!

Finally I would like to mention another young man who has made me laugh – and not just once. He seems to have drifted from comedy lately and has become one of our leading musical stars – but he does one of the best impersonations of me that I have ever seen. He began his career doing excellent impersonations and gags and is a very funny man. His talent stretched to having a good singing voice and hence he has gone into musical shows. Take a bow, Gary Wilmot – you are a star!

We don't all have the same sense of humour and that's all to the good isn't it?

We all have different styles of laughing as well, from the controlled titter to the explosive guffaw. My laugh was captured on a record in the 1950s and that was a very successful number but also, something of an accident!

I was at a recording studio in St John's Wood in 1952, and I heard that Joyce Grenfell was also recording in the same building. I wanted to go and have a chat so, when there was a tea break, I went along to see her. She was also having a break so we nattered over our cups. In the corner of the studio her pianist began tinkering and went into the tune that we now know to be *Narcissus*. It goes: "Dah dum, dah dum, da-da-da da-da-da dee-dum!" Altogether now! "Dah dum Dah dum, da-da-da da-da-da dee-dum!" That's it! You've got it!

Anyway as we talked, Joyce began to "Dah dum" along with the tune. I joined in and we had a great laugh about it. Record producer, Norman Newell, said we ought to record exactly what we had just done. Three days later we did just that with the resulting *Narcissus – The Laughing Record* which is still being played today, near enough forty-five years on!

Well, you have to laugh, don't you?

Such Is Life

"REGRETS... I've had a few!"... That's how the line goes in a well-known song and, like everyone else who has lived such an eventful life, I can look back and pick out a couple of things that I regret having done – or not having done! However, in general they are far outweighed by the things that I have enjoyed doing.

One of my regrets is in not seeing the danger of trying to keep a marriage afloat while I was working on the other side of the Atlantic. In retrospect, I should have either put my marriage before my career and stayed in Britain, or come to some arrangement whereby my family could be with me in the United States. It was stretching things just a little too far by trying to keep both plates spinning at the same time. It was inevitable that, eventually, one or the other would come crashing down. It was a great pity that it happened and, even though we did remain friends, I do regret the loss of Freda.

There is another regret that I have never mentioned before. Some years ago I was offered a television series but I turned it down. On reflection it would have been an ideal vehicle for my sort of humour and I wish that I had agreed to it at the time. In the event, the series proved to be a huge success and, as for the young man who did do it, he went on from being well-known in this country to international stardom. I must say that he really deserved that stardom because he tackled the part superbly and has thoroughly deserved every ounce of his success and fame. I am talking about Michael Crawford and the series that I really regret turning down – *Some Mothers Do 'Ave 'Em!*

Of course, I have made many more mistakes in my life than just these – but these are two that I really regret. Most mistakes give you at least something to salvage and, if you never make a mistake, you never learn anything! – I have had my share!

On the brighter side, I have had many great experiences that would never have been a part of my wildest dreams when I was a kid. Who ever would have looked at that ragged little street urchin all those years ago and said, "You are going to grow up to be a film star and meet the Queen!" They would surely have been committed to an asylum for even thinking of such a possibility.

I have also met many interesting people, some of whom I have already mentioned. As an example, when I was first starting I appeared in a charity show with the legendary George Robey. He was a very, very old man then and, as he worked, his wife prompted him from the wings. Even so, it was still a joy to have been on the same stage with him. To a young comic with hope and ambition it was a real confidence booster to actually be rubbing shoulders with someone like George Robey.

There was another great George whom I have already mentioned in previous pages – George Formby! George, if you recall, stepped in to replace Donald Peers in our summer show in Blackpool. It was another part of my education to be on the same bill as a star like George Formby. He and Beryl, his wife, kept themselves mostly to themselves and lived only a short drive from the theatre, so we didn't see as much of them as I would have liked. Having said that, we did chat quite a number of times and I found them to be a friendly couple. Much has been said about them not getting along together, but there was no evidence of that at Blackpool. George was the performer and Beryl took care of him. It seemed to work for them!

George was much loved by his audiences – and why not? His songs were always full of fun, enthusiasm and optimism. He had the sort of personality that instantly warmed an audience before he ever did anything.

When I was in America I met Edward G.Robinson. He was one of the many stars who surprised me by knocking on my dressing-room door when I was in the States. Here in Britain, Edward G.Robinson was renowned as a villain in Hollywood gangster films but, like James Cagney, he was a very talented man who was equally well-known in the States for many other roles – often as the good guy! He was an all-round actor whom I found to be a perfect gentleman with a marvellous personality, a quick sense of humour and totally the opposite of the hard-faced, ruthless villain that he has portrayed in so many of his films.

I once had another unusual experience one morning when I was in my Kensington office-cum-flat. The phone rang and I snatched it up. "Allo!" I answered, with a voice I often use when I'm in a hurry.

"Hello Mr Wisdom!... It's Cary Grant here!" came the reply.

My mind raced quickly through a whole list of possible suspects who might be trying to do a not-very-good impersonation of the great film star. I decided to play along with it!

"Oh yes Mr Grant!" My voice took on a 'tiffin with the officers' kind of tone. "How can I help you?"

"I wanted to call round to see you – would about half-an-hour be all right?"

"Of course! I'll put the kettle on and you can bring the biscuits," I said, still stalling as I tried to guess who it really was."

The phone clicked off.

About half-an-hour later there was a ring at the doorbell. I rushed to the door, flung it open and prepared to confront the perpetrator of the joke. I stopped with a jolt at the person standing there. It was Cary Grant – THE Cary Grant!

We had a coffee – no! He didn't bring the biscuits! – and he explained that he had come to see me on behalf of Warwick Films of America.

"They are very interested in you," he assured me. "Who's your agent?"

I gave him the details, we finished our coffees, and he left.

Not too long after that I received another phone call – this time from Billy Marsh – who said that he had got a phone call from some nutter pretending to be Cary Grant who was trying to arrange for us both to go for a meeting with Warwick Films the next morning.

We did go to the meeting and there we met two highly-polished executives. A deal was struck and we waited for a script to arrive. Eventually, it did come and it was absolute rubbish! About eight months after that the deal finally evaporated altogether. It cost me about £2,000 to have solicitors look at various contracts and yet, in the end, there was nothing to show for it.

I never saw Cary Grant again after that initial meeting, and it is still a mystery to me, even now, why he was representing Warwick Films, why he never made any sort of contact again and, most of all, why he never brought the biscuits!

Dame Vera Lynn must be one of the best-loved Britons of all time. You've already heard about what she did for me at the Victoria Palace, but we met again on many various occasions since then and she remains as lovely as ever! Vera is a tireless worker for charity and whatever little time she does get to herself she likes to put to good use, taking an active interest in her village, the local WI, and similar groups. She sings as well as she ever did and it wouldn't surprise me if she was singing just as well when the centenary of VE Day is commemorated in 2045!

Vera is one of the all-time greats!

Jimmy Durante is another star who had a great sense of humour. We had a lot of laughs when we met. His comedy and his style of singing were unique to him and I often wonder how many people realise just what a great musician he was. I've said it before and I'll say it again – if you'll forgive me – they don't make 'em like that any more!

Before you begin to accuse me of being nothing but a name-dropper, let me explain that to people in showbusiness, meeting other people in the business is no different to a group of plumbers meeting other plumbers or to a group of white-collar workers meeting together for a chat. We all respect the other one's talents but we rarely look upon each other as stars.

One of my favourite ways of rubbing shoulders with mates is by attending functions of the Grand Order of Water Rats. It is an odd thing, but most people seem to have heard of the Water Rats and yet few seem to know what they are about. Membership has to be proposed and approved and it is chiefly open to performers or those who are closely associated.

The Water Rats stage all kinds of events as well as having regular lodge meetings. Their events are all fund-raising efforts. Various charities are helped but one of the main functions of the Grand Order of Water Rats is to help fellow entertainers in need. We all know what it is like to fall on hard times. The Water Rats have provision for helping those who are financially troubled. It is all done with extreme confidentiality and is a nice arrangement that has been there to give people a leg up when it is most useful.

I am delighted to be a member and I attend as often as I can. It is a light-hearted organisation but it has helped many people through heavy situations.

I belong to various other organisations and I help a wide range of charities as much as I can. Whatever I do, it always feels such a very insignificant bit – but I do my best!

Being involved with charities and various organisations means that you get asked to many different luncheons, dinners, receptions and so on. Usually, the catering at these events is truly excellent but, to be honest, I'd rather have something simple. People often think that I am joking when they suggest meeting for lunch because I like to eat out, just as I would at home – with very basic cooking!

If Johnny Mans and I are having a business chat over lunch, I usually suggest that we visit a MacDonald's or something similar. I think that I embarrass people at times because I like to have a laugh when I'm out. Usually I get recognised when we are in a MacDonald's or a Burger King or somewhere like that, and so I mess about a bit. The trouble is that not everyone that I have to meet for lunch can take it. Another problem is that sometimes there are foreign staff who have never heard of me, and when I mess about they think that I am some sort of nutcase who has wandered in off the street.

My favourite is a Whopper Cheeseburger and chips with an orange juice to help it down. If I don't like something that is on the plate, then I put it on someone else's plate while they are not looking. I'm just a big kid really! Another favourite trick is to get everyone to stand, distract them, and then change seats so that someone finishes up sitting on my knee or on the floor. I did that at a BASCA Awards ceremony once and caught out Roy Castle. He didn't stop laughing over it for the rest of the evening.

Another time I went to a reception at a very, very posh hotel in London, after Johnny Mans had been made a Freeman of the City of London. This place was so posh that even the Queen wouldn't get in without a tie! The group of us were sitting waiting for our food which seemed to be taking ages. I was starving, so finally I went into the kitchen, picked up some plates of sandwiches, put them on a tray and did my stuff as a waiter. The staff were both horrified and in hysterics. I think that one or two of them would have liked to have told me off but I got away with it.

I can't help wanting to have a laugh – and I was hungry too!

I was once taken for a meal at the famous L'Escargot restaurant in the West End of London. It is a very exclusive restaurant with an excellent menu and first-class service. The only problem was that I wanted egg and chips. Incredibly, they were shocked and wanted me to try something else, but I really did want egg and chips. They gave in and served me my egg and chips – and very nice they were too! The next problem was that I like ginger beer and the restaurant didn't have any. A waiter was sent to buy some and this poor chap had to tour Soho asking people for a 'ginger beer'! Now anyone who understands rhyming slang will tell you that walking around Soho looking for a 'ginger beer' is not a very good idea! However, that hardy waiter returned after about twenty minutes looking like someone who had just won the Tour De France. He had found the ginger beer and had returned unscathed!

Once, at an Italian restaurant, I encountered a chef who was extremely proud of his cuisine. He used to tour the tables virtually daring anyone not to finish every morsel that was in front of them. Johnny Mans was in the group, which also included Barry Cryer, David Lodge and David Graham, and I ordered this kind of Italian chicken pie. According to John it was excellent and he finished his in no time at all. It was far too rich for me, so I chose my moment, and I swapped plates with John. I was in the nick of time! Seconds later, the chef had appeared and proceeded to castigate a helpless Johnny Mans for insulting him by not finishing his meal!

Simpson's, in The Strand, is another wonderful restaurant. It used to be a gentleman's club – you know, the sort of place that Phineas Fogg would have been in before he did his tour of the world in eighty days! Today it is a superb restaurant, although I do think that the management will probably have a much lower opinion of me than I do of them! Simpson's takes great pride in fresh salmon. It is served almost before it is off the hook. I prefer the tinned stuff, though, and when I was there I only wanted John West's salmon! The management remained very calm, tried to persuade me, but then sent out for some when they discovered that I wouldn't budge. They must have thought that I was a pain in the neck – and I probably was – but I don't see the sense in paying to have something that you don't really want.

Have you seen those high tables that are in some burger-bars? They are usually surrounded by a sort of sloping perch that you lean back on rather than sit on. They can be a real problem for a little bloke like me! The first time that I encountered them was in a very busy West End burger-bar. I wasn't tall enough to lean back on the seats so I tried to jump up and sit on one. Every time I landed I slipped off again because of the slope. In the end I had to borrow an ordinary chair and sit at the table in that. Then I found that it was quite a job reaching up to the table to eat my meal. The rest of the customers were in hysterics – I can't imagine why!

I don't always win in these situations either! Sometimes the laugh is completely on me. I have made many radio appearances during the decades and, when I was asked to go to the BBC's Broadcasting House, I was really looking forward to it. It will be great to be back among so many old friends, I thought, people whom I know and people who really knew me. I strutted into reception enjoying every moment of being back in such familiar surroundings.

I smiled at the receptionist.

"Yes?" There wasn't a flicker of recognition in her face. I told her who I was there to see. She made an enquiry over the phone and then told me which floor to go to. Just as I turned to leave she called me back.

"Hang on a minute – you've got to wear one of these!" She handed me a security badge upon which she had written my name... 'NORMAN WILSON'!

It is not always that difficult. On another occasion I was going to the Motor Show at Earl's Court. Johnny Mans was driving and also in the car were his son, Elliot, and Elliot's pal, Derek. As we approached the exhibition centre the traffic was horrendous and John threw a panic about parking.

"Don't worry!... Just do as I say," I soothed him. John wasn't too sure – especially when I told him to drive right inside the building.

"We can't go in there," he protested – but I insisted that he did. There was a security guard at the entrance. I wound down the window and smiled at him.

"Hello! I'm Norman Wisdom and we've got a bit of a problem. We've been stuck in the traffic and I'm here to do a very important interview in about two minutes. Now we don't know where to park!"

"Don't worry!" The security guard could not have been more helpful. "You can park here! Nobody will bother you!"

John stopped the car and I issued my last instruction: "When we get out... run like mad! We're supposed to be late!"

So we piled out of the car and sprinted all the way into the hall. Once inside we stopped to catch our breath. "There! I told you not to worry!" I grinned triumphantly at John.

"Just as long as we don't have to sprint out again later!" He gasped.

I'm sure it won't be long before he's on the same Drambuie 'medicine' as was Billy Marsh!

He might not be the only one. I was in London to be interviewed on LBC Radio by Michael Parkinson on one occasion. The *Daily Telegraph* asked if they could send someone along to the studio and also ask me a few questions. Once again Johnny Mans was with me and we arrived quite early in order to do the *Telegraph* interview before going on air with Parkie. About twenty minutes after the appointed time there was a call from reception to say that a young lady from the *Daily Telegraph* had arrived to interview me. I was waiting outside the studio and so John went round to fetch her. When he arrived back with her I was sound asleep!

"I'm terribly sorry to be so late," apologised the reporter. "I was caught up in the traffic!"

"Well, he's fallen asleep now," whispered John. "We had better wait for a few minutes rather than wake him. He's not getting any younger you know!"

"I understand," said the young lady, also lowering her voice. "I really am sorry."

"Don't worry about it! I'll tell you what – just go and sit next to him and then, when he wakes up, he will see that you are there!"

John then made himself scarce while the reporter sat herself carefully next to me. After about three minutes of absolute silence, I suddenly let out a great screeching yell. The girl scream-ed and fell off the seat on to the floor, whereupon John reap-peared from his hiding place and I, all at once fully awake, was grinning all over my face at her.

"I'll bet you won't be late again," I laughed, and she had to agree. In fairness it wasn't her fault that she was late anyway and she did take the joke very well indeed!

I have been caught out myself a few times. Two of these times were on very public occasions as I was twice the subject of *This Is Your Life*. On neither occasion did I have any idea that any-thing was about to happen. The researchers for the programme are very good and it is extremely rare for the secret to be leaked.

To give you some idea of what it is like, imagine that you are walking along the road with your mind totally into something when, suddenly, someone stops you in your tracks and says: "Hello!... Do you remember me?"

That is what it is like when you think that you are about to attend a function only to find that, from out of a group of people, you are accosted by someone who is vaguely familiar holding a microphone and with one hand behind his back. Behind his back, of course, is that famous red book. When you are in show-business you get used to people approaching you with micro-phones so that in itself doesn't mean a lot. Then, when the red book appears and the penny finally drops, it comes as a real shock!

Once you have recovered from the initial shock, the fear begins to set in. You are afraid that there may be someone that you would rather not meet! Even worse than that is the fear that you might upset someone who you can't recognise or remember. My butterflies were with me again throughout the first pro-gramme and then, when it happened a second time, they had all had babies! The second time, you are sure that even though you got away with it the first time you are bound to slip up now!

I am happy to report that I didn't slip up on either occasion.

I have a good memory for voices and faces and it did not let me down either time. After the show you have a nice get-together. Everyone has relaxed by then and it is really good to chat and reminisce. Later on, when you are alone again, you reflect on what has happened and remember some of the people who were missing from the line-up.

If I happened to be a subject of *This Is Your Life* for a third time, I know I would miss Billy Marsh who, sadly, passed away in 1995. There are other family members and friends who are no longer with us – but rather than dwell on the sadness of their absence, I prefer to let my mind relive the happy times when they were here.

My mother had a wonderful little verse which I learned by heart as a child. I have recited it to myself countless times over the years – and I still do! It goes like this:

> "Such is life, and life is such
>
> And, after all, it isn't much.
>
> First a cradle, then a hearse,
>
> It might have been better –
>
> But it could have been worse!"

My Mates

THERE have been times when I thought that I did not have a friend in the world. When I walked to Wales and was deserted by the lad that I had gone with I felt very lonely indeed. When I sat alone in the hostel on Christmas Day 1929, the mashed potatoes on my plate became sodden and salty from the tears that I just could not keep back. Life can sometimes be very cruel can't it?

Showbusiness was the silver lining in the dark clouds of my early years. It gave me income, travel, experiences and many, many wonderful friends. The Army did give me these things to a degree but it was showbusiness that took over and gave me my life!

During the years I have met thousands of people. I forget very few. Yes, sometimes the faces and the names are difficult to match – but I rarely forget anyone.

I have already mentioned some of my friends – people like Pat Dickinson, David Lodge, Johnny Mans and many others – but among the people I count as true friends are those who come to see me at the theatres or at special appearances. Yes, when I say that making a stage appearance is, to me, like entertaining friends, I really do mean that! The effort that people make to come and see me is greatly appreciated. I do not forget my early years and I count every friend as an item of precious jewellery.

As well as those people who come to the theatre to see me, there are many others who just say a few nice things to me when they see me in the street. Every time that I am asked to sign an autograph, I feel that I've made yet another friend. Imagine how it would have been all those years ago, when I was a grocer's errand boy, if someone had said, "Hello Norman! How are you? Can I have your autograph?" I could never, in those far-off days, have ever imagined such a thing happening to me.

When I was even younger, nursing the bruises from the latest good hiding from my dad, I assumed that whatever the problem was between us, it was all my fault and I probably didn't deserve the affection for which I craved. Now, I really do feel and appreciate the affection that is shown to me by so many kind people.

As well as people coming up to me in the street to chat and shake hands, I also receive many letters. I do try to answer them but it is not easy and so, if anyone has written to me and has not yet received a reply, I hope that you will accept this as a public thank you and an apology for not having responded directly.

Every day I receive a shoal of mail from all over the world which I make a point of reading personally. Even if you have had no reply from me, you can rest assured that I have read every letter or card that I have ever received.

I thought that you might be interested to see some of the lovely letters that I receive and I have picked up a small selection at random to reproduce here. I hope you enjoy reading them and sharing in the lovely sentiments expressed as much as I did when I first received them:

Kingswinford
West Midlands

Dearest Norman,

May I start by saying it is great to know that you are making another movie. It was great to see you on the news about your new film. I have waited so long to get in touch with you. I have admired you as an actor since I have been eight years of age. I have all of your films, books, and what would fulfil my long time ambition would be to meet you.

On some days when I wake up and it's a very dismal day, the children are playing up, I just put on one of your videos and it cheers me up no end.

I don't think that anybody on this earth can put sunshine back into my day like you do. I am 33 years of age. I have two children, 10 years and 14 years and a 47-year-old husband. He remembers your film *The Square Peg* as being your first film. He went to see it at the pictures. I think if he's honest with himself that's his favourite.

I must admit that I love all of them but if somebody asks me if I've got a favourite one, it would have to be *A Stitch In Time*. I have read your books two and three times over. First and second time I read *Don't Laugh At Me* I cried over and over again, it was wonderful. I am so pleased that from a very, what seems to me as being a very hard childhood, you have been so very successful.

You have women cooing over your Mel Gibson, Arni's, Richard Gere of this life but they will never have what you have – style, class and most of all you have got what it takes to make a very dull day into a ray of sunshine. You will always be my 'Man of the Moment'.

Norman, I am closing now because I have said what I needed to say. I want to wish you all the best in life and maybe, just maybe, one day I will get to meet you

God bless you,

Best wishes,

Take care

from your No 1 fan

Melanie Beardmore

Bolton
Lancashire

Dear Mr Mans
I write to ask a huge favour.

My close friend VERONICA MCDONALD is arguably
the biggest Norman Wisdom fan on the face of this
planet. She sees him perform whenever she can and is the
proud owner of every film that he's ever made.

She is a wonderful friend to me and I know that
she would treasure Mr Wisdom's autograph, so I write to
ask if it would be possible for you to send it to me, as I
would love to give it to her at Christmas or for her birthday next year.

I appreciate how busy your schedule must be and I
thank you so much for your time.

Lisa Allen

Brighouse
W Yorks

Dear Mr Norman Wisdom,
On reading the *Yorkshire Post* yesterday, 13th Sept,
I saw a picture of you and some girls – you're making a
new film. I want to say how I love your films and have
taped some to keep but I haven't them all unfortunately.
But if the BBC put you on again I'll tape the films. I think
you are a lovely person and I have not met you but I
would love to. I watched *Last of the Summer Wine* filmed
not too far from where I live, wished I'd have known, I
would have come to see you. I have a six-year-old

daughter named Danielle who loves you too. Please Norman, would you let us see you when you're in Yorkshire again?

With all our good wishes

Amanda Brayshaw and Family.
PS Could you sign me a lovely picture.

Plymouth
Devon

Dear Mr Wisdom,

I have been a very, very big fan of yours since I was a kid and have seen and collected nearly every film you have made, my all-time favourite being *The Square Peg* and *Trouble In Store*.

I love the scene in *The Square Peg* when you are working in the road nearby to an Army camp, where they are marching to orders given by their drill sergeant, and you keep on popping out of your hole to give them different orders, to which the end result is side-splitting.

To me you are the best comic actor ever to grace our screens.

I do have but one request. I would dearly love a signed photo of yourself.

Darren Martin

Spalding
Lincs

Dear Norman,

Just a very quick note to you to let you know how

much pleasure you've brought my wife and I over the years and to ask a very big favour of you please. You are truly one of the greatest comedians the world has ever seen and it is great that you are doing a new film. Our family have all been big fans of yours for a very long time and my father managed to get your autograph many years ago in Boston, Lincs.

Can I be really cheeky and ask a very big favour of you please? Would it be possible for you to send me two of your autographs? The reason for this somewhat strange request is that I would love to frame one and hang it on our study wall. The other I would like to keep safely tucked away so the sun can't fade it.

Thank you so much for taking the time to read my short note as I can guess you are a very busy person. I really hope you can help me with my request as it would mean so much to all of us. Best wishes to you and thanks for bringing so much joy to us all over the years.

Yours Sincerely
Deane Baker

Comber
County Down

Dear Mr Wisdom,

I enjoy all of your films very much and you have many fans here in Northern Ireland. I am writing to ask you, if you could please send me an autographed photo of yourself.

Thank you for taking the time to read my letter.

Best wishes
Pearly Rose

These are typical of the hundreds of letters that I receive each month and I am sure that the pals who have written them will not mind me sharing them with you. I appreciate them a great deal and I am sure that you can understand why.

It has been a long road from Paddington to the Isle of Man, and I really have no complaints about the journey. For every unkind person in my life there have been thousands of lovely people. I know that I could call on any one of you at any time if I were in need of a cup of tea. I know that you'd soon have the kettle boiling. That means an awful lot to a one-time no-hoper street urchin from the back-streets of London.

Thank you all.

Whatever Next?

ONE of the questions that seems to come up most often is about retirement. Have I retired? Will I retire? When will I retire? I have never, in all honesty, seriously answered these questions but there is a first time for everything. Before delving into that though, I do have some new projects which might interest you!

When you get a little older you tend not to rush into things at quite the same rate. As I sit in my conservatory here on the Isle of Man, I sometimes like to reflect on past experiences and challenges. I never understood the meaning of words like 'no' or 'can't' in the past. If ever I was asked if I could do something, I was always saying 'yes', even before they had finished speaking. I have to say that my eagerness often let me in for some difficult, and sometimes scary, moments.

I remember putting my entire career on the line on more than one occasion, simply because I was unable to resist a challenge. When I was in America with *Walking Happy*, there was a critic called Walter Kerr who was known in the States as 'The Butcher of Broadway'! Now there was a man who could close a show after a single night simply by giving it a bad write-up. He could also make an artiste's career terminally ill in exactly the same way.

I was warned about him before we opened with *Walking Happy* but I took little notice. With me, you always get what you see. I don't believe in pandering to people just to make sure that they are not unkind to you. Anyway, I took the risk and it paid off for me. The so-called 'Butcher of Broadway' turned out to be a real gent.

"Now we've got him here, let's hold on to him and never let him go!"

That was one of the things that Walter Kerr said about me. It surprised a great many people who had assumed that, because I was a little English guy and it would make better copy to pull me down, I was bound to get a bad write-up from him. Instead he gave me a real pat on the back. My career was far from impeded by my American adventure – the gamble had been a successful one!

It is also a bit of a gamble when you agree to tour overseas. When you look at some of the places that I have visited that 'bit of a gamble begins to look more like a game of Russian roulette, in which you use a chamberful of bullets instead of just the one! We have already talked about Iran, but there were also trips to such places as Thailand, Singapore, Hong Kong and other parts of the Far East, Moscow, New Zealand and Canada. Each trip has represented a different, and very real, challenge. You gamble your reputation and your personal confidence each time. If I am going to do a show in Inverness, Plymouth, Cardiff or King's Lynn, I know that I am going to be among friends. When you venture abroad, especially to some areas which have at times been considered hostile, you can never be sure of what to expect. If an audience in Bangkok doesn't like you – where do you go from there?

These are all challenges and, whatever else, they certainly get the adrenalin going. I am no angel but I no longer rush in quite so recklessly as I have done in the past. I pause for a deep breath nowadays – and then I rush in!

Years ago, when I had only been in this wonderful business

for a few months, I was appearing at Brighton. A message came to the dressing-room asking me if I would go to the theatre bar as a Mr Max Miller would like to meet me.

Max Miller!... Wow!!

I went up to the bar and we shook hands.

"I've watched you Norman, you're very good! Have a drink," he said.

"Thanks, no disrespect, but I don't drink!"

"Don't drink eh? Well you've got to have something with us – what about a cider? That can't do you any harm!"

I thought about it for seconds. I still had the second show of the evening to do, but cider was practically non-alcoholic so that shouldn't be a problem. At least that's what I thought! I had my glass of cider and we chatted. That was the most potent glass of cider that I have ever had in my entire life. By the time I went on stage I was definitely half-cut – if not three-quarters. Instead of just doing my falls, I was launching myself about six feet in the air before crashing down on the stage floor. It is no wonder that I went really well that night.

It almost taught me a lesson! Max had offered me a drink as a gesture of goodwill. He could never have realised that I was just not used to any form of alcoholic intake. I didn't even realise that cider WAS alcoholic. When we chatted his words were very encouraging, but I didn't take them in very well because my brain had become like blotting paper absorbing the cider. I could well have wrecked my career that night by messing up my act in front of the best house of the week. My instinct had been to stick with the lemonade that I usually drank, but I didn't listen!

I always pay attention to my instincts now and however much logic may point to my taking a certain decision, I always allow that special 'gut feeling' to have the final word. These days, more than at any other time, I let my instincts rule my life and I will only develop those projects which feel right.

What kind of projects? Well, at the end of 1996 there will be the British theatre tour and the filming of *Adam and Evil*, the black comedy that I mentioned earlier in the book. That has been on the drawing-board for a long time and it now looks as if it is going to happen at last. I believe that there will be some filming in England and some in Ireland. If all goes well it will be released in the latter part of 1997, it will break all box-office records and take every film award in existence with me picking up about fifty Oscars!!

Ambitious?... What, me?

I have another film up my sleeve, if some nice, kind producer would like to take me up on it. It is called *He Who Laughs Last* and it is really a three-quarter length silent film which follows a day in the life of a tramp – from the minute that he is awoken from his slumber, on a park-bench beneath his Fleet-Street designer sheets – commonly referred to as newspapers, by the dawn chorus. By the time that he returns to his 'open-plan' bedroom, he has had a glorious and satisfying day thanks to his living off his wits. People who have seen the script tell me that it could be a classic along the lines of *The Plank*. It is available for television, films, masonics, jumble sales and school speech days!

A few years ago I did a radio series called *Robbing Hood*, in which I played the part of a burglar funded by a member of the aristocracy, played by Moira Lister. Now, there is interest in turning it into a television series. After the success of *Last of the Summer Wine* and *One Foot in the Grave*, perhaps the TV powers-that-be have finally realised that it is quite possible to have British shows which include people who are well past puberty. I would love to do *Robbing Hood* but that is not my only television ambition. There is a soap that I would like to appear in.

Norman Wisdom in *Neighbours*? Surely not?

It could, and would, happen if I was offered the chance. I have visited Australia many times during my world tours and I would jump at the chance to return for perhaps a brief cameo role in the series.

I love Australia and Australians. It's been about eight years since I was last there but I believe that my films are still being shown on Australian television from time to time. I have always said that they have impeccable taste!

When I go there, they love to see the act. Some of them have seen me in Britain and like to have a chat after the show or even when I'm walking in the street. They are such a friendly people and I have very fond memories of Perth and Adelaide in particular.

A friend of mine from the Isle of Man, Duggie Martin, a builder by trade, emigrated to Perth a few years ago. It would be great to see him again. Yes, I would love another trip to Australia and I would be really thrilled to play a guest role in *Neighbours*. I do watch it when I can and I think that it is a nice, light drama. Perhaps I could be in a couple of episodes as someone's accident-prone English uncle? That would suit me down to the ground.

I believe that the quality of Australian productions has risen steadily over the years and that's why I would welcome the chance to do something there. I'm sitting by the phone waiting for the right offer – just as long as they don't want someone who is tall and good-looking!

My most recent album of songs is called *Nobody's Fool*, and was released by Carlton. I have recorded many songs over the years and I have written about fifty myself. I enjoy song-writing because it is another great aspect of creativity. It is the perfect valve for the release of all those emotions that life mixes up inside you. All the top composers were barmy they tell me! How am I doing?

As well as writing songs, I like to write scripts. Like most ideas, few ever get much further than a box-file on the shelf – but I still enjoy putting them together. I have penned just about everything, from quick sketches to full-scale productions with a cast of thousands. One of the advantages of living in a quiet spot on the Isle of Man is that it is peaceful and your brain can kick its heels without having to contend with noisy traffic or non-stop knocking at the door.

I haven't yet answered the questions at the beginning of this final chapter, have I?

Be patient! I'm enjoying myself. One of my problems is that I like to be busy. When I took a break a few years ago, everyone thought that I had died. The same thing happened when I went on an extensive world tour in the 1970s. I was away for ages and when I got back to England a lot of people thought that they were seeing a ghost!

When I am touring, there are some people who come to see the show at every theatre on the itinerary. It is lovely to see them there every night. I wonder how they will feel if they read this book and see that I have decided to tell the public that I am retiring at the end of 1996. After this year there will be no more tours, no more films, no more television, no more radio – nothing! A clean break!

I have earned enough to suffer in comfort, so that's the end of it all!

You should see your faces!

'Norman Wisdom Retires!' is one newspaper headline that you will never see. In theory I have already 'retired' – but I'm not a retiring sort of person and I still cannot resist having a go at anything that comes up. When I'm on stage doing my act I'm not really working – I'm having fun with my mates. How could I possibly retire from having such fun?

What about all those charities that I work for? I've hardly started with them yet! If I can do just one person a little bit of good I will willingly go on working for another hundred years.

All right... I know! So I'm eighty-one, and I'll be eighty-two next February. You are as young as you feel and I feel as if I'm in my forties at most. I can still do my same act and I can still come back for more. The only bus-pass for me is when I am out jogging and I overtake them!!

My life would be totally incomplete without the adrenalin that comes from working, without the joy of meeting people, hearing their laughter, their cheers and that wonderfully unique sound of a happy audience applauding, clapping their hands to say, "we love you Norman".

It makes me happy and my smile too says, "Really? Well, I love you too – with all my heart!"

I enjoy life on the Isle of Man, I enjoy playing in charity golf tournaments, and I certainly enjoy the fun and fraternity of my friends in the Grand Order of Water Rats, Comic Heritage and all those other organisations that are such a part of my life.

I have many fond memories.

"Just call me Duke – everyone else does," said John Wayne.

"I've never heard you sing before," said Richard Burton.

"I don't know how to tell you this," said Billy Marsh.

"You'll be a fool if you don't try," said Rex Harrison.

"My name's Connery, Sean Connery," said James Bond.

"What on earth do you think you are doing?" Said Noel Coward.

"How about this for an encore," said Joan Crawford.

"I'd like you to do a show for me," said Richard Rodgers.

"Don't you think I should go on last," said James Mason.

"Nurse, what's this man doing out of bed?" said Patrick Cargill.

"I don't think that sounds very funny," said Bruce Forsyth.

"You little tinker," said the Queen Mother.

"I'll never be able to sing looking like this," said Howard Keel.

"This lad's going t'be the biggest comedian in Britain", said Gracie Fields.

"How nice to see you again," said Her Majesty the Queen.

"Young man, one day you will be following in my footsteps," said Charlie Chaplin.

They are all echoes from the past, memories that no one can ever steal from my mind.

Why do I want to go on for ever?... 'Cos I'm a Fool!

I want to thank all my friends for all their support – and that means each and every one of you who has ever applauded me in any way. I have been asked how I would like to be remembered, but I cannot really answer that because it is the choice of others to remember me as they will.

One thing though, when people look at my headstone, years from now, I would love them to say, "Blimey!... Wasn't he old!"

Perhaps, as a gentle breeze frolics across the Isle of Man, through the studios of Pinewood and up past the steps of the London Palladium, people will pause and wonder, imagining that they have heard the distant sound of my voice, saying words that will for ever tug playfully at their heart-strings –

"MR GRIMSDALE!!!"

Thanks Norm!

Norman thought that was the end of the book!

Here is a little surprise that he knew nothing about until he was handed the completed copy on the day of publication.

As you can imagine, Norman is one of the best-loved, and most-respected, people in the entire world of entertainment. He is adored by both showbiz folk and just about everyone else who likes to have a laugh!

There were a number of people who asked if there would be an opportunity in *'Cos I'm A Fool* to pay tribute to him. Since the book is Norman telling his own story, it would have been difficult to integrate too many of these tributes into the mainstream of the text without it looking like down-to-earth Norman had suddenly developed a dose of swollen ego.

Rest assured that Norman Wisdom is still the same ordinary bloke that he has always been. There are no airs and graces – what you see is what you get! Nevertheless, in this surprise section of the book there are a few tributes from just some of those who were really insistent…

JOHN FISHER
(major TV producer.)

Norman Wisdom was the first star I ever met. In the autumn of 1956 I found myself entering a competition published in a children's comic called *Mickey Mouse Weekly*. I can barely remember what I had to do to take part – something about matching the names of characters to their pantomimes, making sure that Widow Twankey did not pester Dick Whittington and that Abanazer kept out of the orbit of Humpty-Dumpty. To this I had to add a line or two explaining why I wanted to win. The prize said it all – a trip to the London Palladium to see Norman Wisdom in pantomime with a behind-the-scenes visit to meet this shrunken-suited, cap-crowned king of comedy. To a bespectacled youth in short trousers, the likelihood of winning was as far-fetched as Christmas in August but, one day late in November, a telegram was duly delivered to our house with the news that would magic me to Argyll Street in London's theatre-land a few days before Christmas.

The production, an ornate confection by that grand master of spectacle, Robert Nesbitt, was a version of the Aladdin story re-christened *The Wonderful Lamp*. Apart from its distinctive title and production values, which I have not seen matched in pantomime since, what made this show newsworthy was the fact that Norman played Aladdin himself, to my knowledge the first time the principal boy had been played by a man in a traditional show.

During the interval I was escorted, together with the other two prize winners, into the wood-panelled splendour of the Palladium's number one dressing-room to meet my special comic hero. I would learn in later years that meeting your heroes is not always a good idea – they can tend to disappoint! However, to this wide-eyed kid from the provinces, Norman showed nothing but friendliness and warmth at a time when he would have been under pressures I could not have understood. This was the FIRST night!

Little did I know then that in later years I would not only meet Norman again but work with him on a number of occasions. There are many qualities I admire in him, not least his versatility and physical agility, his vitality and enthusiasm, as well as a painstaking perfectionism. Nevertheless, it is still that same warmth and human concern that impressed a schoolboy all those years ago, coupled with an extraordinary ordinariness, that come to the fore – making him just about the most humble star I know. Perhaps this is why his star continues to shine so bright.

I often wonder how much that first visit to see our greatest knockabout clown at our most famous theatre played a part in steering my life and career along the course it finally took. In all the times I have met Norman as an adult, I have not told him – until now – about that childhood meeting. It also seems as good an opportunity as ever to say thank you.

JOHNNY MANS

How can a person describe Norman Wisdom? He is everything to everyone! Norman is undoubtedly our greatest living clown. He is an accomplished dramatic actor, a prolific singer/song-writer, a playwright and a comic genius.

He is also my own and my family's best friend.

Over the years of knowing him our working relationship has gone from strength to strength and has become a way of life from which a bond of loyalty and trust exists, essential in any business association.

On a personal level he has become part of our daily life which has enriched every waking day. He is father, brother, uncle and son, all rolled into one. My children long for his regular telephone calls which bring not only humour, but also help and advice should they require it.

His charitable work is endless, raising thousands of pounds for the Grand Order of Water Rats, the Entertainment Artistes Benevolent Fund, Mencap, Comic Heritage, Aspire, British Heart Foundation and many, many others.

As a performer he is a legend... but, above all, he is a wonderful human being.

MAX BYGRAVES

Norman Wisdom and I have known each other for many, many years and have actually worked together. I have seen how he can bring an audience to its feet. I'm glad he's written this book because there was so much more I didn't know.

BRUCE FORSYTH

In all my years in the business, I can honestly say that the two *Palladium* TV shows with Norman were the most hard, the most hazardous and the most horrendous I have ever experienced!

By the way, I have never had so much fun – the little tyrant!

JOE PASQUALE

Norman Wisdom has been my hero for years. He is probably the funniest man I have ever seen. I have seen him perform many times but it was only recently that we met for the first time and he was exactly as I had hoped – down to earth and naturally funny! I was appearing at Epsom Playhouse and he visited me at the theatre. He came into my dressing-room as if we had been next-door neighbours for years and told me that he had written a few songs for his next film. Then he began singing them to me. I thought, 'I've got this legend in my dressing-room singing to me', – I couldn't believe it!

Norman is simply Norman – the little man with a big smile for everyone. To me he is Norman Wisdom, a living legend of comedy. What a fantastic man! Cheers Norman!

ERNIE WISE

Norman has been a friend for years, but it's not that friendship that motivates me to pay tribute – it is admiration. He is an example to everyone who wants to make it in showbusiness. His comedy is honest and and genuinely funny. He is a tremendously hard-working man who has kept himself very fit. He is still one of the biggest box-office attractions in the business even after all these years.

Whenever we are together he makes me laugh. We have often appeared at special functions together and have immediately been on the same wave-length. It would have been nice to have done a few shows together with me as his straightman just so that I could have had the privilege of saying that I had worked with the two funniest men in showbusiness.

Norman, you have been a great friend and a real star. Please keep it up for many more years.

RAY ALAN

I'm sure that Lord Charles will not mind me saying that we have both been big fans of Norman's for many, many years. When you think of Norman Wisdom's achievements it poses a real problem because there is never enough time to discuss all the things that he has done and it is very difficult to think of anything that he hasn't done.

Strangely enough, the first time that Norman and I ever met was in a supermarket in Epsom. He is one of those people that you always feel you've known for years and when we met it was like seeing an old friend – which, hopefully, is now the case. He is a wonderful person and a great entertainer.

JIMMY CRICKET

Norman Wisdom is the master of comedy! He is hilariously funny and no matter how many times you see him he still makes you laugh. He is very fit and supple, which means that his movements are still fantastic and help paint the picture that he so brilliantly creates... And there's more! Norman is a lovely man. He is always totally approachable and, when you think that he has been a star for about forty-five years, it is a tribute in itself to a man who not only has enormous talent but has an enormous heart as well!

PAUL DANIELS

When I was 19 and staying in Hong Kong I saw an enormous queue of people. I walked along the line until I could see what it was that they were queuing for so eagerly. It was Norman Wisdom films being shown around the clock. The season went on for ages I understand. There are very few entertainers who could sustain that sort of appeal, but Norman did and has!

Although we knew each other, the first time that we actually managed to sit and chat was on a cruise ship. He spent some time talking about different comedy routines and anecdotes and he had Debbie and myself rolling about with laughter.

At the Water Rats Lodge, it is customary that if a member has not been able to attend for a while he stands up and gives us a little talk about his adventures since we last met. When Norman did this, he went through all the motions and gestures without actually saying anything. It was hilarious and he had his fellow entertainers in hysterics – especially when, after about twelve minutes, he said, "…and that's what I've been doing," and sat down! I've never seen anything like it – but that's Norman Wisdom!"

CHARLIE DAZE

Norman is perfection in the art of making people laugh. I love to watch his films over and over again. It is not easy for a comic to make other comics laugh – but Norman has that great talent. When I was on *The Comedians*, television did a lot for the stand-up comic – but Norman was going years before that and he is still going years afterward. He is a lesson in laughter-making. I do not readily use the word 'legend' – but how else can you describe Norman Wisdom. He is a fantastic man!

GERRY MARSDEN

Norman Wisdom is, without doubt, the funniest guy I have ever seen. As a singer myself I have also taken a great interest in his vocal abilities.

He is great! Norman would make and sell records, albums, videos, the lot – even if he was not so highly successful as a comic. He can really sing. I think it's high time we did an album together – that should ruin his career!

Seriously, Norman Wisdom has to be one of – if not THE,

greatest entertainers this country has ever produced. Not only that but he is a really nice bloke. Long may he reign!

BERNIE CLIFTON

Norman Wisdom is the funniest thing on two legs. He's a brilliantly funny man who has an almost unique ability to be as hilarious on stage as he is in his films. He has a marvellous singing voice as well and it all adds up to a man who has done it all, done it better than just about everyone else — and is still doing it!

Norman is a national institution. His films are still being shown all over the world and he has fans in just about every country that you can think of. Personally I think that he is a riot — and he is such a nice, down-to-earth guy. Keep doing it Norman, we need you!

DAVID LODGE

I appeared with Norman in many of his classic films and hope to be in many more with him. I was also in his first-ever television series so, as you can imagine, we have become close friends. Norman is also a brother Water Rat and I was very touched that, when I was initiated twenty-six years ago, Norman went out of his way to be there, even though his mother had died just two days earlier. It was not out of disrespect for his mother, far from it. It was just that he is a very loyal and true friend and wanted to be there for my special day.

I have made about 115 films and my happiest have been while working with Norman. He is a great entertainer, a nice man and a great mate.

DAVID GRAHAM
(Comic Heritage)

In 1996, Norman Wisdom is our annual president and that has given me a great opportunity to spend more time in his company. He is simply one of the nicest people that I've ever met and as an entertainer he is a British institution. Whoever said that life begins at forty, or that life ends at seventy, must have been reckoning without Norman Wisdom. He has pushed back the barriers of age, nationality and prejudice simply by making people laugh. What a wonderful man!

GORDON LORENZ
(Norman's Record Producer)

Working with Norman Wisdom is like working with no other person in showbusiness. He is one of those rare people who can do a take and get it right first time almost every time. The trouble is that he is such a perfectionist that he likes to do several takes to make sure he has it right. We almost always go back to the first one. If there is ever a flaw in the first take, I have a sneaking suspicion that he does it on purpose to justify doing it again.

One problem with Norman is that he rarely stays serious for very long. It is a problem keeping him in the record booth. Once he has done a take he comes out of the booth and starts joking about with the orchestra and playing their instruments. It can get quite hilarious and it is left to the poor record producer to sort out the chaos. I wouldn't have it any other way.

On Norman's *Nobody's Fool* album you will see a track entitled *Old Fashioned Lady*. It is a song that Norman particularly wanted to record because it was taught him by his mother when he was a boy. We searched everywhere for the words and music and drew a complete blank. Norman, however, remembers the words and sang them into a tape without any backing. We then wrote the music from his singing. It was quite an amazing experience to hear this 80-year-old man remembering and singing words that his mother had tought him when he was a little boy.

That is what working with Norman Wisdom is like – an amazing, wonderful experience that makes you feel both thrilled and honoured to have enjoyed.

BERNARD BALE

It was in 1954, when I was eight years old, that I was bundled into a coach with about fifty other people and taken across London to see an ice show. There was a man in that show who had me screaming with laughter. That same man had me laughing 'fit to bust' when I saw him in *Trouble In Store* and a series of other great films of that era. I laughed again when I saw him more recently in a large theatre – a theatre which had 'sold out' weeks before his arrival. My own laughter was drowned by the sheer volume of laughter from his audience.

On behalf of all the millions of people who have had their lives enriched by the little man in the tight suit and flat cap – thanks Norman!

Index